A POSITIVE JOURNEY

ERIC D SAYCE

Working with Dorcas on a tactile plan

A POSITIVE JOURNEY

ERIC D SAYCE

THE DOG ROSE PRESS
LUDLOW
ENGLAND 2013

PART 1 - THE LIGHT GOES OUT

First published by the Dog Rose Press of Ludlow, England in 2013
83 Greenacres, Ludlow, Shropshire, SY8 1LZ, UK

Printed and bound by Orphans Press Ltd,
Leominster, Herefordshire

ISBN 978-0-9528367-6-6

Printed and published in the United Kingdom.
Date of publication 2013

DEDICATION

I wish to dedicate my story to my first best friend, my German Shepherd Guide Dog Dorcas who in her own way opened so many doors and made so many friends for me. She gave me confidence to live a near normal life and participate in activities I had not thought possible.

To my grand children Samuel, Joseph and Hannah who have been my motivation for writing this book.

To my wife Jean, daughter Nicola and all my friends who are too many to mention by name who have supported and encouraged me to achieve the things I have. To you all – thank you.

ACKNOWLEDGEMENTS
Janet Smart for her interest and support for this book
Terry Stone for proofing yet another book
Caroline Morris for reading the manuscript and encouraging its publication
To Andrew Fox and Newsteam for allowing the use of their photographs

PREFACE

At the age of fifty my life changed direction. I became blind, it was a shock, something that I had not anticipated but which was to change my perception of life, relationships and bring me closer to God. My story details the trauma experienced by both my family and myself in adjusting to this new life. It describes how I learnt to live my life again and the kind of adjustments which had to be made to enable this to happen.

The story covers the early years of my life as a blind person and is written with humour as well as being punctuated with reflections which are sad, because becoming blind is like suffering a bereavement and one has lost a part of one's body that can never be replaced.

The purpose of writing my story is to raise the awareness in my sighted friends of the potential we all have, whether we are experiencing a disability or not, and how we can best exploit that potential to its full. To my visually impaired friends I hope that my experiences will help allay the fears that you have and motivate you to take that one step further, "OPEN THE DOOR" and enjoy the life that is available to YOU.

My story traces the initial trauma of becoming blind, learning new daily living skills, getting out and about with the use of a long cane and a most important contributor to my confidence and independence, my best friend, my German Shepherd Guide Dog, Dorcas.

In Part 2, Learning to Live again, read how I begin to explore and test the limiting factors created by my disability. My other senses are rediscovered and exploited.

Writing my story has, I believe, been the best therapy for me. It has enabled me to completely open my door and enjoy the real world.

CONTENTS

PART ONE - The light goes out

Dedication and Acknowledgements

Preface

CHAPTER 1
Trauma - My life changes direction

CHAPTER 2
More operations, more trauma

CHAPTER 3
We move house, I take early retirement

CHAPTER 4
I am registered blind, coping with my blindness

CHAPTER 5
Tears of joy, tears of sorrow

CHAPTER 6
I learn to live again

CHAPTER 7
Mobility, the long cane version

CHAPTER 8
Mobility, the Guide Dog way

PART TWO - Learning to Live again

PREFACE TO PART TWO BY THE DOG ROSE TRUST

UPDATE

Since writing this account of my early experiences, a number of years have passed before I had the courage to publish it. Initially I wrote it as it proved to be good therapy for me, but also to leave for my grandchildren a record of what happened to Grandpa, why was he blind, how did it happen and what caused it..

In the intervening years huge advances have taken place thanks to largely the development of the micro chip technology (IT) and improved public awareness of the needs of the blind and partially sighted.

Among the areas which have benefited from this technology are daily living skills, mobility and leisure. Whilst I benefited from the services and equipment available at the time, compared with today's equipment availability they were very basic, but nevertheless they enabled me to gain in confidence and independence.

I list just a few examples of how today's development and the use of this technology is assisting in the improvement of the quality of life of we blind and partially sighted people.

Daily Living
Digital voice recorders help in note-taking, recording telephone conversation, making shopping lists and so on. Talking telephones, both land line and mobile, assist communication providing, in addition to the normal voice to voice facility, texting and access to information via the internet and e-mail, G P satellite navigation and many other facilities are being added all the time.

Personal administration; the use of a computer fitted with software such as the facility to produce large characters on the screen or the use of a voice synthesiser which reads the information displayed on the screen with an almost human voice has greatly improved our independence. When a printer and scanner are connected to the computer, sending and receiving sighted information is no longer a problem.

In the kitchen there are talking microwave ovens, talking weighing scales and liquid measuring jugs are available along with talking tin lids and talking bar code readers.

Personal: talking watches now combine time and calendar announcements at the press of a button, bar code labels with bar code reader machines make the choice of clothes much easier; talking buttons which can be sewn onto clothing are also available for this purpose. Talking colour meters which confirm the colour of a garment are also assisting one to ensure one is correctly dressed.

Leisure: talking books and music are available on CDs, Daisy CDs and memory sticks which can be accommodated in the normal computers, talking book machines and specially designed radios and players.

Audio description is available on the television, in the theatre and cinema. This system allows a description of what is happening to be relayed to the viewer in between the spoken dialogue of the film or play. Audio guides with tactile plans are making museums, heritage sites, country walks and historic buildings accessible.

Mobility – talking GPS navigation systems designed for the blind and partially sighted are available; talking real time information at bus stops is available with the use of a special key fob type gadget.

Guide Dogs for the Blind Association
It should be noted that the systems employed by GDBA in both the training of the dogs and the Guide Dog owners are constantly reviewed and improved. Many changes have taken place since training with my first guide dog, Dorcas. I mention just a few: student's no longer reside at the training centres when training with their dogs and hotel accommodation is now used or as an alternative domiciliary. This is where the student remains at home and training is carried out from home using local routes which the student uses every day or a combination of both hotel and domiciliary. The Guide Dog is introduced to the student in the students home environment and often left with student over a day or so to see how the pair get on. Choke chain collars are no longer used.

CHAPTER 1

TRAUMA - MY LIFE CHANGES DIRECTION

Thursday, June 13th 1985 started off as an ordinary day; it was not a Friday, which for some people could have been the explanation for what was about to happen to me. I remember the day as though it was only yesterday: cloudy, bright, dry and warm. I was employed as a sales executive for an international company manufacturing plastics raw material ABS (acrylonitrile, butadiene, styrene) with the trade name Cycolac to be precise.

I had been working in the UK for the last six months having spent the previous three years selling on the export side of the business. I had visited such countries as Eire, South Africa, Israel, Portugal, Sweden and Spain, a fact which, later in my life I count myself as having been very privileged to have experienced.

My plan for the day, after following up some business enquiries in Bicester, was to visit an old friend, a customer, with whom I had built a good relationship, having achieved sole supplier status when I was UK sales manager prior to my spell in the export field. The company was called Hozelok and they were situated in the little village of Haddenham, just outside Aylesbury. Hozelok manufactured high quality lawn sprinkler systems with a wide range of water hose fittings and gardening equipment, all of which used ABS in their manufacture. I had

In my office at work

renewed my contact with them during the six months that I had been back in the UK with a view to retrieving the business. With this in mind, we had just produced a colour match for a green colour for a new product for which I was confidently anticipating securing a first 20 tonne order.

I was contemplating this as I was driving my car between Bicester and Aylesbury, along the good long straight stretches which once formed part of a Roman road. It was a fairly quiet road, not very much traffic about, when my attention was suddenly drawn to a glider being towed up into the air from a nearby glider field. I watched the glider momentarily and wondered if my friend from Long and Hambly at High Wycombe was at the controls. I knew he was on holiday and being a keen glider pilot was planning to spend his time flying. It was only a brief glance as obviously my attention was needed on the road, but when my eyes returned to the road I felt what I thought was a little bit of grit in my left eye. I blinked my eyes a couple of times expecting it to disappear, but it didn't and it began to become a little bit irksome.

I pulled into the next lay-by in order to check where this foreign body was and then to remove it. The car came to rest, I applied the handbrake, turned off the engine, took out my clean pocket handkerchief and looked into the car interior mirror. I was expecting to see a dead fly, but as hard as I looked I could not see anything. I judged that whatever it was had probably been flushed out by me blinking my eyes and that what I could feel was the soreness caused from where it had been. Satisfied, I proceeded on my way. As I drove an uneasy feeling began to creep over me. I felt that something was not quite right as the vision in my left eye seemed strange.

My appointment with Hozelok was not until after lunch and as it was only around 11.30 I had plenty of time, the whole lunch hour in fact. To keep myself occupied I decided to explore the new industrial estates on the approach to Aylesbury. I turned into the estate and began to nose around but my heart was suddenly not in it. My left eye began to play up again and now I thought I could see what I can only describe as rainbow coloured rings in my eye. These rings appeared like oil slicks; you know the kind of effect that you get when a drop of oil or petrol is dropped into a puddle of water in the road, it spreads a thin film over the surface of the water giving rainbow coloured rings at its edges, like those caused when a stone is dropped into the same puddle, a ripple effect. I blinked my eye but they were still there, they did not want to go away so I decided not to make any more cold calls but to find a nice quiet lay-by where I could have a sandwich and relax, which I did. Sliding my seat back and dropping its back to the near horizontal position I closed my eyes and rested for three quarters of an hour. When I opened my eyes I hoped that all would be okay again, but it wasn't. Those damned rings were still there, but now there were three of them. I rested for another three quarters of an hour by which time I had to be on the move again if I was going to make my appointment with time to spare.

I remembered that there was a telephone box in the centre of Haddenham village which was normally quiet with plenty of parking space, so I decided that if my eye was no better when I got there I would telephone my eye consultant, Mr Groves, and seek his advice and reassurance. This seemed logical because the previous day I had been to see him for my biannual check up; I was short sighted and have worn glasses since the age of five. During his series of tests I remembered that he had used various eye drops in order to dilate the pupil in my eye. Maybe there was a possibility of some foreign body getting into my eye off the end of the dropper and maybe it had dissolved during the intervening period and was now the cause of my discomfort.

Having made my decision I pulled out of the lay-by and proceeded on my way. My vision was fairly clear, I mean I could see through my eye and things appeared in focus; it just seemed to have this hazy film effect floating about. As I approached Haddenham from the Aylesbury direction, there was a long straight stretch of country road and it was along this stretch that I began to realise that these oil rings which were floating about had now been joined by five big black blobs which were in a vertical line across my vision. At that stage I couldn't get to the phone box fast enough. Thank goodness the phone box was empty and in minutes I was speaking to Mr. Groves and explaining my predicament. Having listened to my description he assessed that I had experienced a small haemorrhage in the eye and that providing that I could see quite clearly there was no need for me to worry, there wasn't a problem. These little black blobs would disappear over a period of months; if they didn't, then I was to go and see him.

Feeling very relieved I left the phone box and drove on to keep my appointment with Hozelok, now concentrating on the business in hand, securing that order and obtaining colour samples of the other colours which our competitors were supplying. The business discussions went well and I achieved the order and collected samples for our colour lab to match. Once or twice during the interview, which lasted for just over two hours, I noticed that the buyer seemed to go out of focus; it was only momentarily so I pushed it to the back of my mind convincing myself that I was just being silly.

Business having been completed I returned to the car intending to drive home via Banbury. Within minutes I realised that my eye was not right, in fact it was very wrong. I could now see lots of what appeared to be little 'tadpoles' swimming around in my left eye. This obviously reduced the amount of light entering the eye, so things seemed to be dark, like it is at dusk although what I could see was quite sharp. Decision time! Should I continue to drive home or should I turn back and try to find the accident unit at Aylesbury hospital? To find the hospital in Aylesbury was going to be difficult, I wasn't sure that there was one and I certainly didn't know where it was situated. The time was 16.30 and the beginning of the rush hour. I knew that I would be involved in quite heavy traffic and not being sure of my way I would encounter lots of difficulties. The way home was across open country, with quiet roads except for Banbury, but there I was familiar with a short cut which I knew like the back of my hand so I would not have to drive through the town centre. I also remembered where the telephone boxes were from which I could phone Mr Groves and acquaint him with my latest situation which was causing me a great deal of concern.

I decided to drive home. 'Sod's law', as they say, the telephone boxes, normally quiet and accessible, were now either vandalised or someone was using them. At last I found one on the approach to a petrol station on the left hand side of the road, at the top of the hill near the hospital, as you enter Banbury. The time was now nearing 17.15. Would Mr Groves still be there? No he wasn't, but his secretary was. She listened to my expression of concern and made an appointment for me to see Mr Groves in the morning at 9.30. I continued on my journey home taking it very steady; it was, thankfully, without incident. On arrival home I told Jean, my wife, of the day's events and about my appointment with Mr Groves next morning. I didn't feel like having dinner, but went straight to bed instead where I lay flat on my back and tried to rest. Later I was to learn that this was the most sensible thing to have done, but at the time however I was finding it very difficult to relax. I tried to keep my eyes closed but found myself frequently opening my left eye, making comparisons: has it got any worse? It seemed that the next morning would never come.

THE NEXT STAGE

Friday morning 14th June 1985, overnight a few more 'tadpole-like' impressions had joined those already resident in my eye, but now I was in Mr Groves' consulting room and he was examining my eye. After only what seemed to be the very briefest of looks he drew his chair back and said, "Right, we need to get you into hospital quickly for an emergency operation, you have a detached retina."

My heart leapt. I was dazed with the shock of this announcement: what is the retina? Will the operation be successful? Will it hurt? I really didn't fancy an operation on my eye. In the background I could hear him talking to Jean on the telephone telling her that he was trying to make arrangements for me to go into hospital. I was worried, how would she take the news? In a daze I heard him telling me that he was not prepared to do the operation himself as it appeared to be delicate and complicated, but he knew of other consultants specialising in the retina field whom he was recommending. He was talking about me having to travel to London to Moorfields Eye Hospital, but was not happy with the distance and time it would take to get there. He stressed that I was to be extremely careful from now on until I was in hospital as the retina was in a critical position and it only needed the slightest knock or jar to dislodge it completely. "Walk on eggshells" was the expression he used to frighten me to death, thus ensuring I took note of his bidding.

"Miss Eagling is the person for you", he said. "She is the leading specialist in retina problems and she is based in Birmingham and could do the operation in the Nuffield Hospital Birmingham, that is, if she is available." "Please may she be available", I heard myself saying and then after what seemed to be hundreds of telephone calls the confirmation came, yes she would see me. She would make arrangements for me to enter the Nuffield Hospital in Harbourne Birmingham and would see me at 7.15 that evening. Armed with an introductory letter from Mr Groves I left his surgery, very much in a daze and not fully realising what was happening to me. I drove my car the 2 miles home, very, very carefully bearing in mind the advice I had just been given. My eye was by now much worse and I could hardly see out of it as the 'tadpoles' had nearly taken over completely.

In the meantime Jean had telephoned the office in Leamington and put them in the picture. They kindly arranged to send a hire car over to take me into the Nuffield which was a relief, as I was worried about how I was going to get there as Jean is not a driver. My hospital bag packed, a friendly pat for Pippa, our little Shetland collie, and I was on my way, accompanied by Jean and Nicola, my daughter, who had just sat her GCSE O level history exam that morning; she joined us straight from school. We were all on tenterhooks and the atmosphere was very tense; every time we came to a traffic light junction it was a worry in case the driver had to brake suddenly and the road seemed to have bumps and potholes all over it. I tried to protect my head by cradling it with a pillow as best I could, being very mindful of the advice that I had been given. Finding the hospital was giving our driver problems and I was not helping matters by being impatient and up-tight, consumed by my problem and not being of much assistance to him, but at last we were there.

IN HOSPITAL

At 7.30 that evening my room door opened and in came Miss Eagling, the retina consultant specialist. She was a quiet, unassuming lady, medium height and build with a reassuring manner. One of the nurses brought in a box-like piece of equipment which opened out to reveal an inspection lamp, binocular type lenses and a chin rest. This machine, which I was to learn later and become very familiar with, was called a Slit Lamp. The machine was set up on a table and drops put into both my eyes, one set to dilate them and one set of anaesthetic drops. I then sat in front of the lamp with my chin resting on the chin rest while Miss Eagling focused the binocular-like lenses in towards my eyes through which she could see right into the back of my eye where the retina is located. She instructed me to look in different positions in order to have a most thorough examination.

She confirmed the earlier diagnosis: "Yes, you have a detached retina in the left eye", and that she would make the necessary arrangements to operate on that eye in order to replace the retina. The operation should be straight forward providing that I followed her instructions by lying flat on my back and perfectly still, not moving my head about as the retina could dislodge with the slightest movement. The operation was timed for 9.30 the following morning, Saturday the June 15th 1985. Miss Eagling then departed saying as she left, "See you in the operating theatre in the morning."

Almost immediately the ward Sister came and joined me sitting on the end of my bed. I will always remember her very clearly and never forget her explaining what was going to happen to me, the possibilities and what I could do to help myself; in fact she frightened me to death. I remember thinking to myself "Sister why are you telling me this because I don't really want to know?" and I was getting quite hyped up about it.

Later I learnt that this approach was good psychology because with the retina so delicately balanced I had to lie perfectly still and not move my head around. I was so concerned about the problems that could ensue if I didn't follow this advice that there was no fear of me ignoring it. During my recovery following the operation Sister told me that all the staff were very concerned about me and that if I had not been a good patient and followed their advice they would have had to cradle my head in sandbags, packing them all around me as I lay flat in order to ensure that I could not possibly move my head. She explained how relieved everyone was when I went down to operating theatre that morning because they knew just how difficult it had been.

Needless to say I had little sleep that night, just dozing and worrying about the operation, feeling very lonely and trying to keep my head still which was extremely difficult. I kept getting cramp in my limbs and wanting to move them. There was a notice hung on the bottom of my bed 'nil by mouth', which meant nothing to eat or drink and I was feeling so thirsty. Then at last I heard movement: the ward was becoming alive again even if the time was only 6.30. It won't be long now I thought and then things began to happen as I was prepared for the operation which involved me getting dressed in a white gown which when I put it on was like putting on a coat back to front; my front was completely covered but my back was exposed except for some ties which were supposed to keep it together, but which I had great difficulty in tying.

9.00 and in came the porter with a nurse. The porter was pushing an empty trolley which was to be my carriage down to the operating theatre. Nurse came and checked my arm band which had been applied around my left wrist when I was admitted, making sure I was who the arm band said I was and asking me verbally for good measure. I remember suddenly thinking how terrible it would be if they operated on the wrong eye and then before I could panic we were on the move.

The porter was a good driver and the journey was relatively smooth but noisy. I could hear people walking past me and was aware of passing sister's desk as I could hear her voice giving instructions to someone and then we were in the lift, a noisy metallic barn-like room and quite chilly. The doors closed, the button was depressed and up we went arriving with a gentle thud. During all this time I was lying flat on my back gazing up at the ceiling. I remember the strip lights and how much brighter they were in the anti-room and operating theatre. I could smell the anaesthetic, hear people talking and saw faces peering down at me, heads clad in green tight fitting hats and face masks, only the eyes being visible. I could hear the muffled sound of rubber boots walking about and then I heard Miss Eagling's voice. "Good morning Mr Sayce, how are you feeling this morning?" Before I could reply the anaesthetist was by my left side with his hand holding my left wrist and his fingers rubbing my wrist and back of my left hand with cotton wool. He then asked me to relax and told me that I would feel a little prick which I did and then I would go to sleep. At this stage I remember wondering how long it would take to take effect as I was gazing up at the lights, then I felt my feet going cold and the anaesthetic going round my body.

AFTER THE OPERATION

When I awoke from the anaesthetic I was back in my bed. I remember feeling and being violently sick and then being very concerned that I had made a mess because in my dazed state I had not been able to find the help button. The nurses however were very kind and attentive, obviously quite used to the situation. I had to lie on my left side for what seemed to be an eternity; in fact it was 7 days. This was to ensure that the eye was not shaken, moved or jarred in any way. My eye was covered by an eye shield and bandages which meant that lying on my left side my vision was very restricted. The nurses fed me and gave me drinks using a cup with a spout. Have you ever tried eating and drinking whilst lying in a horizontal position on your left side? Well I don't recommend it. I found it to be very difficult and messy; the food did not seem to want to go down and the urge to turn over and relieve the cramps was almost unbearable and only the fear of causing problems to my eye and the pile of pillows supporting my back prevented me.

My thoughts at this time were constantly focused on the outcome of the operation. I very selfishly prayed over and over again: "Please God may it be successful." Suddenly through my mind went thoughts of all those things that I liked doing: walking in the Dales, photography, driving and wondering if I would still be able to do those things that I enjoyed so much. Would I still be able to see through my eye? I also made a promise to myself that if my sight was restored then I would take a tape recorder with me on my walks in order that I could record my impressions and the actual sounds of the countryside around me and so help give a blind person an idea of its space, freedom and beauty.

I remembered especially the country in and around the Yorkshire Dales and in Ireland, Skibberene and Killarney, recalling the sound of the flute played by James Galway. I had recently bought a copy of his record album and as I relived those visits and heard the music in my head, it all helped me to relax.

The morning the bandages came off I was feeling very, very tense. Would I be able to see? "Please God, please may the operation have been successful, please may I see again." Then they were off, I opened my eyes and yes I could see again. "Oh thank you Lord, thank you," I exclaimed. Yes, I could see,

I could see the light fittings in the ceiling and the cornice where the wall met the ceiling. I could see colours and how fresh they appeared to be. I could see the leaves on the trees waving about in the wind as they were situated just outside my window. It was a marvellous feeling, it really did feel good, I will never forget the relief that I felt. After that initial feeling of euphoria I began to notice that my vision was blurred in that eye, but I was quickly assured that it would settle given time and I was obviously very pleased that everything had been successful.

During my recovery time I remember being very concerned about being able to drive again as my job was dependent upon it. Everyone assured me that providing everything went according to plan there would be no problems. It was stressed, however, that I still needed to be very careful and not bump or jar my head, neither should I bend from the waist, for example, putting my head in a horizontal position. I was, instead to bend from the knees with my body remaining in a vertical position. I was very fortunate that Jean and Nicola were able to visit me in hospital, even having the occasional meal with me, with very little restriction on visiting for them.

It was not easy as neither of them could drive so they depended on public transport and car lifts from friends to get them to the hospital which was situated some 26 miles from Coventry. Obviously they shared the concern over the outcome of my operation, but it was easier for me: I knew how my vision was, what was happening to me and how I felt, but difficult for them as they had to rely on my explanations and advice from the nursing staff. This support helped to keep a positive outlook and reduce those long hours when I was lying on my side. I found that I became very emotional during these initial visits, tearful in fact, which was a little embarrassing. I put the reason down to me being so relieved that I could actually see them again after that period of fearing the worst.

My friends from work kept popping in to see me, cheering me up, checking on my progress and reassuring me that all was well at work. At this time I discovered a new group of friends; they were Jean's friends and in the main from St. Martin's in the Fields Church, our local church in Coventry. I remember Connie Read and Peter Simpson the vicar; I did so appreciate this new-found friendship and support, not just to me but to my family, as it was very reassuring to know that people, many of whom I had never met, were watching over and praying for our family.

CHAPTER 2

MORE OPERATIONS, MORE TRAUMA

During one of my regular visits to Miss Eagling's consulting rooms to monitor the recovery of my eye following the operation, she suggested that I should consider having a minor operation on my other eye, the good one, the operation suggested was called *cryopathy*. The purpose of this operation was to freeze any weak parts of the retina, particularly around the edges and by so doing it would thicken up those areas and thus prevent that which had happened to the retina in my left eye happening to the retina in my right. I was advised that I should seriously consider it and that a bed was available next week. If I did agree then it would mean that I would be over the operation by the time the other eye was better which meant that I should be able to resume work sometime in September.

After due consideration I agreed to do this and consequently went into the Nuffield Hospital Birmingham again on July 31st for this operation which Miss Eagling carried out on the following day August 1st. It was only a minor one, involving a three day stay. The after effects of this operation were, I am pleased to report, minimal.

The time passed slowly and as September approached I began to look forward to being able to work again. Towards the end of August I found myself constantly checking that my eye was still alright. I would do this by closing my good right eye and looking through my left in order to make sure that I could still see everything as I thought I should and then compared it with what I could see in my right eye. I did find that the amount of light entering my left eye appeared to be less than that entering my right; for instance, if I was to look at a white sheet or painted wall through my right eye, then close my right eye and look at it through my left the degree of whiteness wasn't so bright, it was greyer. The same appeared to be true when looking at the television screen. If I was to look at the screen with my right eye it was oblong, but when I looked at it through my left one it was a square. I remember asking Dr Evans, my GP about this and I think he was a little puzzled with my question. He repeated the exercise himself, testing his own eyes, saying, "Yes, the eyes are slightly different, no two eyes are the same". I also asked Miss Eagling the same question but she didn't seem concerned. At the beginning of September, Miss Eagling advised me to make arrangements to have my eyes checked as I would need new prescription lenses for my glasses and I could now consider returning to work.

On Thursday September 6th, the day before I was due to have my eyes tested before returning to work on the following Monday, disaster struck. The retina in my left eye, the one which had previously detached, detached itself again and part of my vision in that eye was immediately lost. The part lost was that part of my field of vision nearest to the bridge of my nose and it was a vertical strip about a third of my vision wide and appeared rather like a strip of wallpaper peeling off a wall.

In the morning of that day I remember doing some weeding in the garden, bending from the knees I must add, as it was a nice warm, sunny day. I had felt something strange whilst I was having lunch with Jean but ignored it because this comparing of the sight in my eyes was beginning to become an obsession. After lunch Jean went off to her meeting with the Mothers' Union and of course it happened whilst she was away. I tried not to panic and called Miss Eagling who was in the operating theatre in Birmingham Eye Hospital at the time I called. She was contacted when she was free and returned my call. I described the situation, whereupon she made arrangements for me to see her in her consulting rooms at 1.30 the following afternoon, advising me to come with a bag packed and prepared for a stay in hospital.

When Jean returned from her meeting she found me lying on the bed in the spare bedroom feeling very tense and trying to keep as still as I could for fear of creating more damage to the eye, remembering very vividly all that the sister had told me prior to my last operation on this eye. That night was a long one; I lay scared out of my mind, afraid of the future and what this set-back meant and scared of undergoing another operation.

Eventually it was morning and time to go and again the same care had to be taken by the driver of the car taking me. I was tense and concerned about every little vibration and bump of the car caused as it travelled over the road surface. Miss Eagling had arranged to see me as an emergency and on arrival at her consulting rooms I was shown into a room on the ground floor, not Miss Eagling's usual one, and asked to lie on a bed.

I didn't have to wait long before Miss Eagling soon appeared and began examining my eye with her special inspection lens/light. Having seen the extent of the detachment, she quickly made arrangements to have me admitted into the Selly Oak

chapter two

Hospital Birmingham, that afternoon, the only hospital where there was a bed available, the intention was to operate on my eye the following Saturday morning. We then drove straight from the consulting rooms to the hospital which was difficult to find and even more difficult to find the block and ward which I had been assigned to. This was not an experience I would like to repeat.

Miss Eagling had explained to me that this operation would not be easy due to the kind of tears which the retina had suffered. She described how she intended to insert a plastic pad behind the eye which would act as a support to the retina and onto which she could flatten it. This support was a small piece of plastic material rather, I imagine, like a suction cup and would be held in place by, for want of a better description, a couple of rubber bands around the eye. In order to ensure that the retina remained flat, she would remove the vitreous from out of the cavity and replace it with a silicon oil which having a higher density would exert slight uniform pressure on the retina and by doing so help keep it in place.

The hospital at Selly Oak was huge and the ward which I was on had around forty patients, the majority of whom were elderly. Many had other disabilities in addition to their eye problems, the majority of which appeared to be mainly cataracts. The nurses were stretched, there being only three of them to cope with all of us. Because of this, I didn't feel there was the same degree of care and interest I had experienced in previous hospitals and with the pressures on the staff I could well understand the reasons for that. I was not very happy there.

Having settled in, the family left and once again I became hyped up with tension and foreboding about the operation which was scheduled for the following morning at 9.30. When morning eventually came so did the anaesthetist. He checked me over and arranged for me to have a tranquilliser tablet to settle my nerves and relax me prior to going down to the operating theatre, which staff nurse duly administered. Guess what? They really did work. I remember taking them and nothing more until I awoke back in my bed after the operation, which in itself was a relief.

On recovering from the anaesthetic I was concerned because my vision was virtually nil in the eye which had been operated on and I had a lot of excruciating pain. Miss Eagling confirmed that the operation had not been easy as the retina did not go back flat. In fact, it had a fold in it and there was also scarring which meant the vision would not be very good. In layman's terms, scarring of the retina is like having a scar on a part of the body which forms when a wound has healed. If that scar is in a hairy area of the body then the hairs do not grow again. Likewise where the healing scars exist on the retina vision will not be regenerated.

The pain in my eye was severe and tablets would not relieve it for more than an hour out of every four. The tablets which gave the best relief were the good old simple Paracetamol, Analgesic and Distelgesic tablets that you put under your tongue and allow to dissolve were all tried. The latter proved quite amusing, although it wasn't at the time. Sister came to my bedside during one of these severe bouts and brimming over with confidence told me that she now had the tablet to put me out of my misery. "It will kill everything; you won't have any pain after you've taken one, just give it 5 minutes." I put it under my tongue and waited patiently, after a quarter of an hour she returned saying, "There you are, I told you it would be all gone."

chapter two

Unfortunately it hadn't. She was obviously very surprised and left me saying, "For you, with pain of that intensity, it will take half an hour, I will be back." Half an hour went by and sister returned; "It's gone now hasn't it?" she enquired, but still the pain thundered on with not the slightest sign of respite. This excruciating pain which I was experiencing was, I believe, caused by pressure on the nerves due to the rearrangement in the eye by introducing the plastic support.

My stay in hospital this time was a week during which my progress was very closely monitored; in addition to Miss Eagling visiting me each evening, daily routine checks were carried out on my eyes by junior doctors, who, I am sorry to say did not impress me one little bit. My impression of them was that they were quite rough in the way they handled patients and quite brusque in their manner.

I do readily admit that I have been very fortunate in having Miss Eagling to look after me, being very conscious of her gentle, caring but thorough manner and delicate touch. Contrast this with one junior doctor who examined my eye one morning, obviously very excited at the prospect. I suppose I was becoming somewhat different from the run-of-the-mill cases due to the damage my retina had caused to itself and the skills of Miss Eagling in performing such a difficult damage limitation exercise. This particular doctor took what seemed to be hours peering into my eye through the slit lamp. The bright light was quite painful and this on top of the constant pressure pain which I was suffering was truly frustrating. She showed no concern or sensitivity to my situation and the discomfort she was causing; she even called over some friends to look at the marvellous work which had been done, but I wasn't even asked if I minded.

A chance remark that Miss Eagling made one evening during her examination of my eye, underlined for me her commitment to her work. I hadn't realised that she was supposed to be on holiday that week and here she was, having come in especially on the Saturday morning to do the operation. During another conversation she amazed me by telling me that during that day she had been laying slabs and concrete in the garden. I obviously thought she had had a contractor in doing the work for her. Next day however, when I asked how the work was progressing, she said that she had had a good idea which had reduced the work considerably. She had hired a concrete mixer! Imagine my surprise and horror when I thought of those skilled fingers with the delicate touch mixing and laying that coarse concrete aggregate.

Another experience I won't forget which happened whilst I was in this hospital, was a fire alarm, a real one. The alarm bells rang and the staff ran to their fire positions. Then I heard the sound of the fire engines in the distance, becoming louder as they drew nearer. In the meantime the hospital alarm continued to sound and we thought we could smell smoke. I remember lying in my bed and, in spite of the reassurances from the staff, feeling very anxious and concerned about just how would we be evacuated and where was the fire. I remember very clearly that there was an outdoor fire escape just outside my door. In the event the fire was quickly contained and confined to a small area in one of the kitchens and fortunately no one was in any danger.

HOME AGAIN BUT WITH VERY LITTLE SIGHT

Was I glad to be home after this operation? Well I won't bother to answer that but unfortunately that excruciating pain in my eye came home with me and remained with me for close on two months. It was a very lowering destructive kind of pain which was close on driving me out of my mind. There was only slight relief for one out of every four hours, but still there were no tablets that would give complete relief. My GP visited and became very concerned about me and prescribed tablets that knocked me out, making me feel like a zombie.

Many, many times I felt like banging my head against the wall in order to release the pressure. I tried audio mind relaxation exercises, even yoga; for short spells I found that kneeling on the floor in the bathroom with my head in the wash hand basin and underneath the cold tap with the latter turned full on allowing the freezing water to flow over my head thus numbing it gave me a very limited relief. In fact I tried anything and everything such was my need. At night the pain would not allow me to sleep. I tried to lie as still as I could for fear of causing further damage to the retina and so as not to disturb Jean too much. I remember breaking out in hot and cold sweats, petrified with the thought of becoming blind and the consequences of that. I needed love and reassurance, I was desperate.

These particular feelings climaxed two nights running in the middle of this period. I hugged Jean, oh how I hugged her, crushing her to me burying my head with all that pain throbbing inside it, into her breasts. It was as if I wanted to melt myself into her. I needed love and warmth to heal that pain.

Then during one of my visits to see Miss Eagling, as she was monitoring developments very closely, she commented that the eye was still very much inflamed and prescribed a large booster dose of steroids with the idea of shocking it into healing. It worked; overnight the pain went. Oh I was so relieved! I felt a completely different person, but that pain, I will never forget. I then went on a course of steroid treatment which continued the healing process and kept that awful pain at bay.

I remember one amusing result which happened while I was taking these steroids. It was a Sunday and I had been quite restless so we all, Jean, Nicola and I, decided to go for a walk before lunch. Our walk took us from where we live along quiet country lanes to the outskirts of Kenilworth, around the southern boundaries of Kenilworth Golf Club returning home through Stoneleigh, a distance of about 5 miles. Two thirds of the way round, first Jean and then Nicola began to flag, whereas I found that I seemed to have a lot more staying power. In fact I had to keep waiting for them to catch me up as I didn't feel as tired as I normally would. Jean and Nicola jokingly suggested that if they could take steroids, then they too would also have been able to perform like me. If the enhancement of my physical output was anything to judge by, then I can well understand why athletes are banned from taking them; for me though, they are the wonder drug.

CONCERN ABOUT MY JOB AND THE FUTURE

During the next 12 months a cataract began to form in my right eye, seriously affecting my vision in that eye. I became increasingly frustrated and anxious about the future. I was not working and my employers were also understandably becoming concerned as they were keeping my job open for me. This was having the effect of putting a heavier work load on my colleagues and making future planning for them very difficult. This situation couldn't be allowed to continue indefinitely, so meetings were called at UK and International Board level. The company were extremely caring both in their approach and negotiations with me, negotiations which culminated with me agreeing to take an early retirement, which I did in August 1986, just fourteen months after it all began.

At the time there really seemed to be no alternative as I could no longer fulfil my sales and marketing role, being unable to drive and service my geographical area. There were no other vacancies in our sales and marketing office at Leamington for which I could be trained, so that was it. After more than 17 years with the company, I found myself, at the age of 51, out of a job and nearly blind.

The tensions generated by the frustrations caused by my sudden loss of vision, culminating now in loss of independence, loss of job and worry about the future, coupled with Jean and Nicola having to step in and take over the responsibilities in the house that I normally looked after myself, was understandably having an effect on them also. Jean had to take over the management of our finances together with all the administration, paperwork and correspondence, something with which she was not familiar, never having been involved. I had always looked after it myself.

OK - I was there to assist with advice on what and how to do it. But I was not being able to clearly see what she was doing and I was not understanding how hard it was for her to just jump in and take over especially under the extra difficulties that I was creating. Eric was not a happy boy at this time; in fact, on reflection, I was a real pig. I was very intolerant, lacked patience and became very angry very quickly. I expected Jean to know where everything was, didn't believe her and argued when she said things weren't where I said they should be. Not being able to see properly and having to rely on my memory when Jean read things to me, especially when filling in the complex forms for sickness and other benefits, caused me to ask Jean to read and repeat what she had just read over and over again until I was sure that I understood its meaning; this was particularly trying her patience too. As a result Jean, who was already a migraine sufferer, found that her attacks were becoming much more frequent and more intense, so much so that she too had to seek help.

When Jean suffered these attacks she was completely immobilised, having to go and lie down in a darkened room for a day or so, which then left me in limbo, increasing my own feelings of uselessness and increasing that feeling of being dependant which I hated. When looking after Jean in these situations, I became very conscious of my difficulties which were severely affecting the way I could care for her at these times when she needed me.

I wondered how she felt now that she had to take responsibility for me, we no longer had that equal partnership. For the rest of my life I was going to be a taker and Jean the giver. Why should she be lumbered with me in this situation? She must be thinking what is the future going to be like for me now? It couldn't have been encouraging as there would be times when she would be in need of tender loving care herself and I felt very inadequate in this respect.

MY RELATIONSHIP WITH MY WIFE AND FAMILY

During these times when Jean was incapacitated I used to become so angry and frustrated with myself. Trying to prepare simple snacks suddenly became very difficult, I didn't seem to be able to do anything without burning or scalding myself, causing a horrendous mess, upsetting things and not being able to find where Jean kept things didn't help the situation. I really used to dread, indeed live in fear, and still do of Jean becoming ill. The problems were exacerbated by Jean herself as she cannot accept the fact that even though I cannot see, I could, with training, learn new techniques such as cooking, and look after us both, especially in emergency situations. I am afraid she sees me as a walking disaster in the kitchen with more food spilt on the floor, work surfaces and hotplate, ruined saucepans and partly cooked meals. In other words, she has a complete lack of confidence in me. Coping with these situations obviously was having an effect, so much so that Jean even tried yoga and special relaxation/massage treatment, in which a friend specialised, providing this service in our home; it helped for a while.

My daughter Nicola

Meanwhile our daughter Nicola was coping with sitting GCSE exams, deciding on her future career which was nursing, something about which she had had firm ideas for a long time now. Looking back, this makes me feel very proud, having experienced the care and attention which I have received from the nurses in the various hospitals during the many operations which I have undergone.

Their presence at so many crucial times has helped to ease the pain and trauma which has gained my respect and admiration.

We were fortunate in a way with the timing of my eye problems coming as they did, with Nicola having decided to leave school preferring to go straight into nursing training rather than sit A levels. However, she had to wait until January 1986 for the training to commence so got a part-time job working in Marks and Spencers, a job which she enjoyed and in which she could have progressed as opportunities were offered to her. I remember the discussions we had; at that stage I wasn't too keen on her going into nursing considering the unsocial hours, physical hard work and poor salaries even for those who reached the top of their profession. For Nicola it was a vocation, something she had wanted to do for a long time and as I have said, I am glad that she stuck with it and became a nurse, which has made me feel a very proud father.

Although I say that the timing could have been worse, it would have been better if it hadn't have happened at all, as it obviously had occurred at a very crucial stage in the development of Nicola's life. The last thing that she needed was to experience all the trauma, worry and lack of support in practical terms that my situation was causing; things like sharing additional responsibilities with Jean, having to move house and suddenly having no family car. This meant getting home from work at the hospital which was situated on the other side of town, late at night on the buses; it was not a thought either she or Jean and I relished.

All this on top of the normal anxiety and concerns that a young teenage girl has at the prospect of leaving the relatively sheltered environment of school and venturing out into the big and very often cruel world in which we all live. I worried a lot about the effect all this would have on Nicola, but she has proved that she is indeed made of stronger stuff; she has been a tower of strength and great support to both Jean and I all the way through and particularly in those early days, travelling back and forth to Birmingham to visit me with Jean on the bus. She helped to calm and sort out the problems at home and gave me those subtle little reassurances that she was keeping an eye on Mum during my frequent stays in hospital. She proved that she had a sensible and caring approach, even if she was churning over inside.

Faced now with the prospect of being blind in my left eye, a cataract growing in my right which was severely restricting the vision in that eye and with the prospect of being unemployed, perhaps even unemployable, it was important that some major decisions had to be made regarding the future. The first was a relatively simple one and one which we made early on.

Our dream house - but we must move

PROBLEMS TO BE FACED - TRANSPORT

The increasing difficulties and eventually my inability to drive was the first change to impact on us. Jean didn't drive: she had been taking driving lessons and had in fact nearly got to the examination level, but our move to live in Coventry had put a halt to any further developments in that area. We did have an old Mini banger when we were living down in Newport Pagnell, Buckinghamshire which Jean used to gain experience in. The Mini came with us to Coventry when we moved, but with all the expense and time consuming jobs that needed to be done around the new house and garden, we never seemed to have the time. Unlike Newport Pagnell, having a 20 minute bus service at the bottom of the road into a good shopping city which Coventry is, removed a major reason for having a second car, plus the old Mini failed its MOT and really was not worth spending money on, so we sold it for scrap receiving the princely sum of £5 for it.

This all happened before my eye problems began; in hindsight, we bitterly regret Jean not progressing with her driving and obtaining her driving licence. With the increasing volume of traffic, parking restrictions and general changes, Jean had now lost her confidence and inclination to learn to drive; as a result we have now had to give up that independence that having your own transport provides, always assuming that in our new environment we could have afforded it.

The future was now reliant on public transport and that's a whole different ball game and many books have been written about the inadequacies of it. Suffice it for me to say, based on our experience, if the partner in a relationship with a blind person can or is willing to learn to drive, and you have or can afford to purchase and run a car, then do it as this is a major key to independence and you won't regret it.

On a more positive note Nicola secured her place on a nursing training course at Walsgrave Hospital Coventry and while we were all delighted, as I have mentioned previously, it did highlight a transport problem. It would involve Nicola in a good deal of bus travel at unsocial hours. The decision was made easy for us: use our savings and buy Nicola a car, a Mini. Her 18th birthday was coming up in October and we had always said that

Nicola in the mini on her birthday

this should be the one to be marked in some extra special way. We did this and as time has confirmed, it was a good decision. For Nicola, hopefully it showed that we did care and she hadn't lost out due to our changed circumstances. It was also a way of both Jean and I showing Nicola our appreciation of her securing a place on nursing training and for the care and support that she had been giving to both of us. One important point, we obviously had to be aware and be careful that we didn't use the car as a means of obligating Nicola to do all our errands for us; it was Nicola's car not ours although helping us with the shopping, taking me back and forth from the hospital was so very useful. I am pleased to say that I cannot recall any problems in this respect.

I remember very clearly that bright October morning, the 14th, I had had the Mini delivered and parked in the garage the evening before while Nicola was out. Jean had decked it out with ribbons and I had managed, with the sight I still had at that stage to make a placard with the inscription *'Congratulations Nicola on your 18th'*. This I had then fixed on the Mini's roof.

That morning I had managed to reverse the Mini out of the garage and under the car port where it waited for Nicola. The look of joy and excitement on Nicola's face when she came out of the house and saw the Mini is one of those moments that I will always treasure. I was glad that I still had reasonable sight in my right eye then because that's a picture that remains very clearly in my mind today.

The cataract growth in my right eye at this stage was not sufficient to prevent me from driving, but in this respect, already having lost the sight in my left eye I realised that I was on borrowed time. I was optimistic that when the cataract had finally developed to the stage when it could be removed then there was a good possibility that I could drive again albeit with one good eye. I was able to sit alongside Nicola in the Mini when she went out to practice. It was very difficult for me; I tried very hard not to let Nicola inherit my bad habits but instead made sure that she received proper driving lessons from a registered qualified driving instructor. Lesley Young, a colleague from the office who had a Mini of her own and several years' driving experience and someone with whom *chapter two*

Nicola related very well, volunteered to go out with Nicola in order that she gained more driving practice.

Nicky stuck with it and in March 1986 passed her driving test at her first attempt. Baptism by fire would be the term I would then use for Nicola's further driving experience as within days of her passing I was back in Birmingham receiving treatment and Nicola was driving Jean back and forth, something that on reflection was good for her because it was a case of, "You don't really have a choice, get on with it." She coped extremely well, not being too inhibited by the fast moving heavy traffic around her in Birmingham; from this experience she has emerged as a very competent driver which has served to be of great benefit to us all.

CHAPTER 3

WE MOVE HOUSE, I TAKE EARLY RETIREMENT

July 1st 1986 we moved house; yes, just thirteen months after that fateful day when the retina in my left eye first detached itself. Prior to that fateful day Jean and I had been looking forward to spending more time together, now that I was back working in the UK. There were going to be lots of opportunities for Jean to accompany me on business trips and with Nicola leaving school and starting work, we would be able to spend the odd weekend away together. Sadly this was not to be, which being philosophical prompts me to reflect, "Forget yesterday, it's happened and one cannot change what's happened. Live for today because tomorrow may never happen."

Our new house in Coventry

chapter three

We had been able to satisfy those preconditions that we had set ourselves for finding a house: it was a pre-war semi-detached one, which had been completely gutted and rebuilt eight years ago, when the previous owners, a young married couple, moved in. It had three bedrooms although the third

The lounge with the view through to the garden

The well laid out garden

bedroom was little more than a box room. The other two were larger than those at our previous house, a small but practical bathroom. It had a nice large airy and light through lounge/ dining room with a brick- built arch divider, a well maintained and efficient central heating system, a large long rear garden well laid out with lawns, trees, shrubs and tall hedges, all of which were long established, making the garden very private. The rear of the house faced the south. The small front garden had been laid to tarmac for the parking of two cars and it had a small lawn with a couple of short flower borders, both gardens being easily manageable. The not so good points were a small galley type kitchen, so we were going to miss our recently installed *Poggenphol* kitchen at our other house. This house had no cloakroom or downstairs loo, the bathroom suite was in a chocolate colour and not to our taste; the detached garage was a wooden one, not very secure and rotten.

The house itself was situated in an avenue lined with lime trees, just off the busy A45 and only one and a half miles from where our other house was situated, so we were still within the parish of St. Martin's and had our friends around us. Only 3 minutes' walk away, at the A45 end of the avenue, there was a small row of useful shops and about 8 minute's walk away was a small post office. The bus stop was at the end of the avenue with buses which took us to the rail station and the centre of Coventry for main shopping; these were also within reasonable walking distance.

We had a large park called the Memorial Park within 5 minutes walk and we were still situated on the Kenilworth side of town not far from Warwick University with the countryside only minutes away. We were well pleased with our choice, a choice which now with the benefit of hindsight, proved to be the correct one. The Lord was surely guiding us because in the light of the developments which were to follow, all those points which I have made relative to our move have proved to be so important and helpful.

chapter three

Moving house is a stressful time for anyone, but for us at this particular time it was especially stressful, something about which both Nicola and I became acutely aware. Jean, having supervised all the packing and loading of our possessions into the removal van, the last minute cleaning of our old house and then taking all our personal and valuables items in the Mini with Nicky to our new house, suddenly went down with a bad migraine attack as soon as the furniture was beginning to be unloaded.

It was a hot dry sunny day; I will always remember putting the deck chair cushions on the lawn behind the trellis screen and underneath the trees, which were providing just a little shade, at the bottom of the garden. Jean was lying down on them with a cold flannel on her head and Pippa, our little Shetland collie, tucking down beside her, safe and out of the way of all that was going on. The light was very bright but there was nothing we could do about it. Jean remained there for the remainder of the afternoon while Nicola and I coped as best we could, directing the removal men to put the boxes and furniture where we thought they should go. The trouble when moving from a detached to semi-detached house is that it is like trying to fit a quart into a pint pot, with the result that we ran out of room. The little garage was packed full and spilt out onto the patio where we had to store many items that should be in the garage. Fortunately I had kept the ground sheets that we used when caravanning so we covered these items up, thus making them weather tight.

My vision at this time was still enabling me to cope relatively well. I had just shadow vision in my left eye and deteriorating hazy vision where the cataract was growing in my right eye, but I felt that I was able to still make a major contribution in the work of establishing our new home. Our plan was to rip out immediately the existing kitchen and redesign it with more effective units incorporating built-in oven and work top hobs, with extractor fan and work light over, built-in washing machine and fridge; the aim was to have a kitchen that was labour saving and provided easy access.

The old garage needed replacing by a double one which would then give me room for a small workbench, some storage space and room to garage Nicola's Mini. Being optimistic we allowed space for a Metro. This needed to be done after the kitchen and before winter set in so as the items stored outside could be brought in.

Coping with all this work was not without its problems. I recall just one situation which concerned cooking while we were without a kitchen which causes us now to smile, but it was a very different tale at the time. We used a camping gas two burner stove to do our cooking, which we did outside in the detached garage, with all the packing cases and loose items all around us and a bucket of water and fire extinguisher at the ready. We were limited though in what we could cook as we didn't have enough burners available at any one time, so we had a brainwave and invested in a pressure cooker. We had never used one before, but once we had mastered the technique we thought it was brilliant and now we could do all our vegetables on one burner at the same time enabling us to still have the other burner free for cooking the main course. Our neighbours, not used to such goings on, had great difficulty in coming to terms at first in realising that the whistle coming periodically from our garage was our pressure cooker letting off steam via the safety valve and that the appetising smells together with the various members of our family suddenly

Preparing to give an after dinner speech

appearing and rushing out into the garage with plates and returning with them plus saucepans, really was down to us preparing our meals. What a relief when the kitchen was completed and we could revert to normality!

RETIREMENT

August 1st 1986, on this day I officially commenced early retirement, just fourteen months after that day when my eye problems began. I certainly had no intention of remaining retired.

Lazing in the pool in South African sunshine

I was planning that after my sight problems had settled and hopefully the cataract successfully removed I would be able to recommence employment, albeit in a different capacity. The fact that we had already taken action to reduce our future living costs would help when it came to my choice of employment, making us less dependent upon the remuneration involved.

It made me feel very sad having to give up my career, a career in which I feel I had been successful and one which I thoroughly enjoyed. I had always felt that I was very lucky to have an occupation which enabled me to travel and meet people, with a large degree of independence, an occupation which provided so many exciting and varied opportunities. I was going to miss all this very much indeed, especially the friends and customers with whom I had built relationships; together we had shared some very difficult and hard times. I hoped that this situation, which had been caused through no fault of my own, would not leave me feeling bitter.

On reflection, I have been very fortunate in that I have visited and worked in many different countries as far apart as Norway, Finland, Sweden, Denmark, Portugal, Spain, Holland, Eire, South Africa, Egypt, Israel, Canada and the United States. I had always been a very keen photographer and used to travel everywhere with my camera gear; it enabled me to build photographic albums of the countries, places and people I had met and visited.

I still have those albums today; they came in useful for Nicola when she was taking her Geography GCSE exams and my grandchildren, Sam, Joe and Hannah, were interested in them too. Although I can no longer see those photographs, I no longer feel sad because I <u>can</u> still see them as they are etched

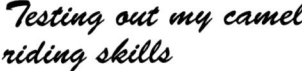

Testing out my camel riding skills

just as clearly in my mind as they were on the day that I took them with the addition that I can still recall the atmosphere and movement. I am lucky because many sighted people have never had, and probably never will have the opportunity to visit and experience the countries, people, and events that I have, all of which are now stored away in my memory ready to be recalled whenever I want.

Time progresses and as it does it has proved that some of my business friends were not just friends influenced by business but real friends interested in me as a person. These friends, particularly those in Sweden, Denmark and the Republic of Ireland, have remained in contact with me over the years, always at Christmas time and whenever they had the opportunity of visiting this country, both writing and telephoning me in order to remain in touch and check on my progress. One good friend in Dublin, with whom I used to work very closely, obviously remembered my liking for smoked Irish salmon, which I reckoned was the best, especially when it was cut so thin that you could see the pattern of the plate on which it was placed through the slice, has been sending me a half of smoked Irish salmon every Christmas since I retired which is now many years ago. The first salmon received after I became registered blind, was already sliced which I found to be both very thoughtful and touching.

MORE TROUBLE WITH MY EYES

During this time I started to record my thoughts about my situation.

> The cataract is now developing rapidly in my right eye and its increasing density is having strange effects. It's almost like sitting in a tunnel and although I can't see detail at the end of the tunnel, the surface of its roof appears very much like the effect of icing on the top of a Christmas cake when it has been whipped up. The rectangular window which was producing a rectangular shaped light area is now becoming much more confusing; it is no longer a rectangle but just a blob. Now in daylight both eyes are producing the same effect. When using a torch however and shining this into the eyes, the cataract eye picks out the light from the torch much more clearly than my left eye, the damaged retina eye. This left eye is seemingly beginning to clear a little now, shadows are beginning to become a little clearer but very distorted, probably being due to the retina not being flat.

Then it happened, suddenly out of the blue, I was plunged once again into darkness. My retina in the right eye, the one with the cataract growing in it, started to detach itself. I was able to make almost immediate contact with Miss Eagling who agreed to see me in Birmingham Eye Hospital. She gave my eye a thorough examination, paused and then confirmed my worst fears, adding that it would be a difficult operation due to the cataract which would now be in the way.

On the January 6th 1987 she carried out the operation involving fitting an encircling band to the eye with buckling support vitrectomy and air exchange. This, however, was unsuccessful in flattening the retina, so on the January 22nd I once again found myself back in the operating theatre for yet another operation. This latest twist in fortune was really heightening the stress levels as I was now practically out of alternatives. If this operation didn't work then that was it. I would be blind and I was scared, oh how I was scared.

I have always been a Christian, but not in recent years a regular church-goer, always believing one is always near God wherever you are, having prayed to him in some very strange places, but now I found myself asking did I only pray to him when I needed something? I needed him now, oh how I needed him. "Please Lord be with Miss Eagling when she performs the operation, please let everything be alright, please let the operation be successful, please be with Jean and Nicola, help them to cope with the worry, please may we all have the strength to face the future whatever it may hold."

On reflection, very selfish wasn't I? What was I prepared to give in return? What was God's purpose behind all this? Did there have to be a purpose? What was he trying to tell me, had I really been so wicked to deserve all this? Finally I offered myself to him to make of me what he would and now as years have progressed, yes, I do feel that there was a purpose behind all this, but read on. I remember enquiring of Miss Eagling, "Will I have to suffer that awful pain again which I experienced after the similar operation was performed in my left eye, because I don't think that I can cope with pain at that level again?" She reassured me that in the light of experience already gained then I should not. No one could have anticipated that cruel twist of fate however and certainly not Miss Eagling, that was to cause a large haemorrhage to occur midway through the operation. The objective was, as previously explained, to exchange the normal vitreous solution in the eye with silicon oil which has an effect like that of blowing up a balloon in the eye and thus being able to exert uniform pressure on the retina, thereby ensuring that it remains flat.

I remember very clearly the build up to that operation, feeling so tense, being aware of the caring, understanding and reassuring attitude of the nurses and the cleaner earlier in the morning down on her hands and knees under my bed; she was an elderly lady but that didn't prevent her dusting the floor and the underside of my bed to make sure that it was spotless, no dust or foreign bodies dared lurk there. I sense that everyone on the ward was aware of the importance of this operation and were with me in their thoughts.

Then, the moment came for the journey on the trolley out of the ward and into the lift, out of the lift and into the preparation room. Suddenly, we were there; nurse did all the normal checks, checking my identity bracelet and other routine actions. The porter who had driven the trolley made me laugh by making some funnies; how is it that all porters who drive hospital patient trolleys seem to have a terrific sense of humour?

chapter three

The operation was timed for 2.30 and we were bang on time. This is it I thought. I could hear the theatre staff bustling around, the clink of air cylinders and metallic clanging of instruments, the smell of the anaesthetic gas. Nurse was standing by the side of the trolley holding my hand, providing a reassuring presence and then I heard Miss Eagling's voice, "Hello Mr Sayce, we're nearly ready for you, the operation shouldn't take too long."

Then the anaesthetist was standing by my side rubbing the back of my hand ready for that needle.

The next thing I was conscious of was lying on my left side in a bed with a raised cot side, everything was dark, my right eye was throbbing and heavily bandaged. I remember being scared, "Oh no, please God, not that pain again, please no." Then I seemed to be fighting to wake up and I kept lapsing back into some deep sleep. I knew that I was back on the ward because I could hear what seemed to be ward-like noises coming from the end of a very long tunnel.

Then I felt a gentle hand on my right shoulder and a voice, it was Miss Eagling saying, "Mr Sayce, can you hear me? I'm sorry Mr Sayce, it wasn't successful," and then it went very quiet with the exception of the pigeons on the window sill outside having an argument over possession of the warmest spot. I felt sad, what did she mean? Was all this for nothing? I cried and lapsed back into a deep sleep. I learnt later that as the operation was nearing the half way stage, the vitreous was being displaced by the silicon oil, when my eye suffered a large haemorrhage which caused Miss Eagling to immediately terminate her work In order to limit the probable damage caused by this sudden haemorrhage. Sister told me later that the theatre staff had said that Miss Eagling had been very upset at this sudden development, which further confirmed my feeling that she really was a very dedicated and caring person. I reckoned that I could understand to some extent how she must have felt; she worked so hard at every stage in the series of treatments to my eyes, always discussing and explaining what she was planning to do, never hurried, always thorough. If anyone could help me, then she was the one.

It must have been so very frustrating for her and no one could have done better; I trusted her completely. I guess she also realised that this development would probably mean that I would experience that pain again, that which she had promised me would not reoccur. The pain was back, not quite so severe and this time Miss Eagling had it under control using those fantastic steroids; it still took its time though. At one stage I went back into hospital for a couple of days' observation, but the inflammation and high pressure still took its time to settle. It was all very lowering. I seemed to be completely consumed by pain; it took over totally.

I will always be grateful to Sister Margaret Perry, who during all this had taken Jean and Nicola on one side during one of their visits to the hospital and had had a quiet word with them, preconditioning them and explaining what was happening. She specifically warned them to anticipate the effect all this trauma and pain, which I had been experiencing over some time now, was going to have on my reactions at home. Sister explained to them that I would probably become very angry and bitter, most of the anger being directed at them; during these times I would appear to become a very different person, a not very nice person.

chapter three

Sister went on to try and reassure them by telling them that it was a common reaction that people experienced when going through these traumatic periods of readjustment and it was far better for all this pent up emotion to be expended this way than being kept bottled up inside which then could give rise to more serious complications. The anger was due to many different things such as the frustration that I felt at not being able to see to do things. At first it would be even such simple things as finding the food on my plate, knocking over drinks, dropping food, being dependent upon others, fear of the unknown, bitterness because they could do things that I couldn't any more, and finally, the realisation that a part of me was lost forever and there was a need to grieve. She went on to explain that this anger whilst directed at them - "You always hurt the one you love"- to always remember that it was not because of anything that they had done, but it was a natural, but unpleasant reaction.

Much later on I was sadly to realise that a very vital component, counselling in the aid of recovery for both patient and family, is not readily available. I and my family were lucky that we had Sister Margaret to talk to and she, through her wide experience, in the limited time at her disposal was able to pre-empt those situations because sure enough they did occur. We were fortunate that she was there for us at this vital time, not everyone is so lucky.

CHAPTER 4

I AM REGISTERED BLIND. COPING WITH MY BLINDNESS

February 6th 1987 I am registered blind. My feelings and the impact that this simple statement had on both me and my family's lives is documented in the following chapters. In order to occupy myself and hopefully promote a positive attitude to my situation, I decided to keep a record of the events and my feelings throughout this period. I used my little pocket memo recording machine to do this; reference back to these tapes has greatly assisted me in writing this book.

I noted one such reference which I recorded on Thursday March 5th 1987 in which I say:

> Today has been a particularly stressful day as there are now positive signs that Jean is having difficulty in coping with the new and double role of both caring for the house, family and planning the changes which are still to be made in the house following our move i.e. the bedroom reorganisation, the bathroom refit and the redecoration of the hall, landing and stairs, all this in addition to the paperwork of the house such as the writing of letters and the settling of bills which I always used to do previously.

My own system of hanging on to all sorts of oddments, such as wood and paint, stowing them away in places where I could find them is now becoming a big problem. Jean is having difficult in locating them. Today for instance, the paint with which to touch up the lounge, I know where I put it and of course I can tell Jean where that is, but it is a different matter when you have to move boxes and equipment to get at it. All those odd pieces of wood, obviously I had ideas where I could use them, such as building blue tit nesting boxes followed by a bird table like that which I built at our previous house. Jean looks on these items as rubbish. I can see her point of view as they are cluttering up the garage and need to be disposed of, which then brings another problem because we have no car big enough to take them to the tip, so we have to rely on other people.

The next day I go on to say:

Similar to yesterday, a very strained situation has existed all day due to Jean's anxiety about her ability to cope, the house being, as she puts it, a tip due to all the work which needs to be done. I feel very frustrated at being dependent upon others. I am not able to do what I want, when I want because it's not always convenient for others to attend to my requirements exactly when I want them, which of course is understandable. I have to learn to be patient and understand that other people have other priorities as well and that these are not necessarily in line with those of mine.

On the subject of frustration, I note that I seem to have poured my heart out into my tape during one particularly low period which I was experiencing at around this time. Prior to my eye problems I was quite a keen DIY man, and of course one of my frustrations now is not being able to attend to the thousand and one jobs which now needed doing around the new house, like, for instance, drilling walls in order to fix shelves and pictures. Even a simple repair to the kitchen waste bin which had become detached from within its housing beat me. I had to try and instruct Jean and Nicola how to do these things which only served to heighten my frustration, because willing as they were, they had no idea how to hold tools and had no experience in doing such things. They had to manage as best they could and suffer me shouting instructions and becoming angrier by the minute which only served to increase the tension between us.

I also found that other people going into my garage to find bits and pieces to do a job, paint and paint brushes for instance, was making me feel angry. In the past I have carefully kept lots of odds and ends, pieces of wood, screws and all manner of little things which, to the normal person and especially to the rest of my family, is so-called junk, but to me they were valuable items which I saved to help me to do a job around the house sometime in the future. I found it very upsetting when the family kept on referring to the garage as full of junk which needed to be cleared out, especially now that I couldn't make use of it anymore and things were always falling over or getting in the way.

As a result of my inability to cope with these situations I began to spend more and more time alone in the little third bedroom which had become my sort of study, somewhere where I could shut myself away from the hurt. In this room I practised my writing and typing, the latter being on Nicola's battered old electric typewriter which I had bought from work when we changed over to on-line computers. Not being able to get out of the house for walks was also frustrating me but I hoped this would change when I started my mobility training.

I referred to being very tired of my own company. I talk a lot about being left on my own when the family go out shopping; when I was sighted we all used to go out together. Now no one seems to think that I would like to go along as well; because I'm blind I suppose there seems little point in taking me, and let's face it I am a liability. In one part of the tape I say:

> There doesn't seem any point in keeping bashing away at this typewriter just to keep occupied, what's going to be the point at the end of it all? I couldn't see what I was typing and asking people to check what I had done became a problem. This afternoon is a lovely afternoon, there's sunshine and it's warm and once again I am on my own. I would have liked to have gone for a walk, in fact I'm tempted to go out on my own, how else am I going to be able to build up my confidence to be able to become independent? Sight is so precious, you don't really appreciate it when you've got it.

I should mention that I am a Samaritan volunteer as this is relevant to the next section of my tape:

> This afternoon, Betty, the director of our Coventry Samaritans branch collected and took me to the Samaritan centre in her car.

> I feel very insecure when outside, the weather was snowing and very cold, I managed OK and even took a telephone call. I found the other volunteers very

helpful giving and offering me whatever assistance I needed, even to the extent of arranging to provide me with transport to collect me and deliver me back to my home. This afternoon Desmond brought me home and stayed for a chat and a cup of tea. Working in the Samaritans is I find good psychologically for me, it helps me realise how fortunate I am when compared with so many of those people who call the Samaritans. My problems pale into insignificance when compared with some of the callers with whom I speak, it certainly helps get things into the right perspective. On Thursday evening Estelle called and took me to a Samaritan group meeting at a private house, which I enjoyed.

This was my first experience of being out with anyone other than members of my family so I was nervous of walking and finding my way around. I needn't have worried because I found people very kind and helpful. I explained that I would hold their arm, they then to lead and me to follow, which worked. I found it strange being in an unfamiliar lounge and hearing people (about 14 in all) talking around me and not being able to see them. I did however find the courage to speak up and put forward my own opinions at what I thought was the opportune time, so I was not as inhibited as I thought I might have been. Helping myself to refreshments wasn't as difficult as I had anticipated either, in that my friends asked me what I would like, having first told me what was available. In this instance I had 2 slices of quiche; my neighbour, Isobel, told me that she had taken a napkin and placed it on my lap. She then took the slices of quiche and put these on a plate and put it on my lap on top of the napkin. She then took a cup of coffee for me drawing a small table up on which to stand it, putting it by the side of my left leg. Eating and drinking coffee in this new group of people didn't present problems for me, these kind of experiences do I feel help to build my confidence levels.

The tape continues:

We had the replacement front door fitted which Jean coped with very well, which, hopefully, will help to give her confidence for the future. Saturday March 7th Jean is very much on edge and anxious; she suffered from a bad headache and pains in her side today. I feel very helpless knowing that I am the cause of the problems. I wish that I was not so dependent. I must try and persevere with my typing in the hope that I may be able to at least start writing letters. My outside activities are strictly limited. Nicola is working and Jean is not very happy about taking me outside; she lacks confidence. Jean is worrying about my forthcoming visit to Birmingham Eye Hospital on Monday, whilst I am confident that I will be OK and need to get out and about gaining experience on buses and trains. Jean is worrying about how she will be able to cope with me.

My first experience of the outside world since becoming blind is frightening. Peter Simpson, our local vicar called the other day, he knocked on the door, Jean was out. I rather unwillingly eventually opened it having made as sure as I could, that I knew the person on the other side, by calling through the door for the caller to identify himself. When I heard the voice saying that he was Peter the vicar, remember that at this time I didn't know the vicar that well but thinking to myself, Peter the vicar? He sounds a nice chap, Yes I will let him in. When I opened the door, what a shock! I couldn't see anyone. It was silly really because I should have been prepared but I still hadn't got used to my blindness. He was standing there, I could hear his voice but I just could not see him. A very important lesson here is to be very careful when opening the door to callers.

The first time I stepped out of the house into the big world outside was equally as frightening. One cannot see anything around you so one loses one's bearings and you don't know where you are. Referring to my tape again:

I feel that this is going to become a major problem for me, I must gain confidence in order to get about but at the moment I have little confidence.

Jean took me out this afternoon to the Day Centre in Earlsdon. I felt very nervous and sensed that Jean was nervous too. The traffic at the major road, the A45, at the bottom of our avenue seemed to be very heavy and noisy, finding kerbs was difficult, shadows seemed to pop up from trees which were situated along the sides of the path which caused me to hesitate. I begin to wonder if I will ever be able to cope, the reason is probably due to in part my lack of knowledge of this area. I had no visual picture in my memory of where we were walking.

chapter four

Another extract from my tape.

> Nicola took me for a walk down our avenue today. I
> seemed better able to cope in that Nicola appeared
> to be more confident. I knew the street in which I was
> walking and Nicola pointed out the obstacles on the way
> and where I was. Sunday March 8th Connie offered to
> take me to the cathedral to a confirmation service but
> because the weather was bad, freezing and snowing we
> declined. Visiting cathedrals and my local church now
> raised a problem. I am no longer able to read a prayer
> book or hymn book and thus may not be able to join in
> the worship and hymn singing; it should not however
> prevent me from participating in the service.

One of my long standing objectives which I made to myself
when my blindness first occurred was that I should learn Braille
and one day when my Braille was good enough maybe read the
lesson one Sunday in St. Martin's church. This was a challenge
for which I could work.

During this time another cataract had been forming on my left
eye, the one in which I had had some light perception but now
with the increasing density of this cataract, all vision had now
really gone, with the exception of the light source areas such
as a torch. Being totally blind was causing me problems with
eating and I found that it was one of the most frustrating things
with which I had to cope.

I also found that sighted people didn't appreciate the difficulties
that blind people experienced. For instance, a blind person
walks into a room and knowing that someone is in the room
calls out "Where are you?" Back comes the reply, "Over here".

"Over where?" again asks the blind person. That reply is meaningless to the blind person isn't it? Is the person by the window, by the table, in the centre of the room, to the blind person's left or right; see what I mean?

Although they probably don't realise it, another infuriating habit some people have, is when they hand you something and when you ask what it is, they will reply, "See if you can tell what it is". Once or twice is okay but when it becomes a quite frequent occurrence, it becomes annoying. I like to know what I am about to eat before I put it into my mouth. Only on a few occasions when we've been attending functions like, a cheese and wine party or a coffee morning have I heard someone asking Jean, "Would he like another glass?" Why they didn't ask me direct I'm not quite sure. Now of course I am much more aware of these situations and promptly reply, "Yes he would, thank you very much" whereupon I get the feeling that the person asking the question stands back in amazement and thinks - hey he can talk.

Another observation I have made is that when one has one disability, like being blind, people generally tend to treat you as though you are completely different. Blindness only involves one's sight: you still have your other senses. You can hear, talk, smell and eat, one's brain still works in the normal way, I think. So why do people tend to treat us as subnormal, incapable of holding an intelligent conversation and having opinions of our own? I also found that people tend not to describe the environment in which one is situated, the choice of food which is available when attending a buffet meal or a self-service restaurant, usually only telling you about the food which they think is good for you or they themselves like.

Likewise when reading the newspaper for you, they choose to read only the items in which they are interested or anticipate are of interest to you, they never read the whole paper. Worse still, if they become absorbed in an item which they are reading to you their voice tails off and then stops because they have become so engrossed in it that they forget that you are there, just as interested as they are, and hanging on every word, which is both very frustrating and annoying.

Another example of this is opening the mail for you. You hear the envelope being opened and the letter being taken out, then total silence, with a perhaps an occasional "Ah!" or "Oh!"; you know that they are reading it to themselves. Why? It is your letter sent to you, not them, how can they be so insensitive?

CHAPTER 5

TEARS OF JOY, TEARS OF SORROW

I experience, sadly only for a limited time, the joy of seeing light and colour again.

> Monday March 9th: today I have to go to Birmingham to meet Miss Eagling. It will be the first time that I will have travelled by bus and by train since becoming blind. Jean was very nervous about the situation and invited Connie to accompany us as moral support. I was quite looking forward to the experience as it was going to get me out of the house and out and about which I badly needed. The day was bitterly cold but dry with some snow still hanging around on the pavements.

Walking to the bus stop was no problem, getting on the bus however was not quite so easy. The bus arrived at the stop but I could not see it, I hadn't a clue where the entrance to the bus was and although Jean advised me I still had no firm idea where the steps were, in fact I walked into the steps. Jean had told me that there were two steps but in fact there was only one, she meant two including the first step on which I was standing, so consequently I made another mistake by looking for the other step and in so doing walking into the driver's cab. The second problem, when I showed my bus pass to the driver I wasn't sure whether it was the right way round or even upside down and as he didn't say anything I didn't know whether he had seen it or not and was he satisfied? Could I proceed and sit down?

I was rescued by Connie who came to me from inside the bus; she took me by the arm and guided me to the first seat whereupon I sat down. Alighting from the bus at the station wasn't a problem as I was able to find both bus steps quite easily. We crossed over the dual carriageway, choosing a point where the middle reservation gave us breathing space. The next hazard was the steps down to the station by the side of the railway lines which I managed by holding on to the rail. It was difficult, however, to find the flat level sections in between the various flights of stairs, but in the end it wasn't such a problem and being led by Jean around and into the station proved all right.

Next obstacle was to gain access to the platform through the ticket barrier; as with the bus driver I wasn't sure whether the ticket inspector had seen my ticket, and orientation once through the barrier was difficult. Next problem was the stairs up and over the rail tracks to platform 4. To negotiate the stairs I held onto the hand rail; in this case it was the outside rail, which meant that I kept walking into corners, it would have been easier to have taken the inside rail and by doing so making the ascent much smoother. Finding the exit hole for platform 4 would have been difficult but as I was being guided it didn't create a problem.

Next encounter was finding the door when the train arrived, but with Jean guiding me we managed alright. Getting onto the train wasn't a problem as I found the steps alright except that when I went into the carriage, I had forgotten that there was a central corridor which I nearly sat down in, thinking there was a seat there. Alighting from the train at New Street Station Birmingham didn't create any difficulties for me, neither did walking with the rest of the passengers from the train whilst I was being guided, then we came to the escalators, which I decided to take and managed alright.

My route from the station to the hospital through the crowded streets wasn't difficult while being led, though at times I was conscious of suddenly flinching as people walked by very close; I was aware of a shadow or a presence. I also noticed the noise around me: people's voices and the various conversations as I passed groups of them. On arrival at the hospital I found that once again stairs appeared to be my major problem. It is difficult to know how many, how deep they are and where the level platforms between flights of stairs are. On my return journey there did not appear to be too many hazards, except the escalators going down initially gave cause for concern because of one tending to lose one's balance and although we returned through the crowded rush hour Jean was able to guide me at normal walking pace, something which impressed Connie who was observing.

On arrival back at Coventry rail station the same problems which we experienced on our way out occurred plus an additional one; on our way from the station to the bus stop, there was lying on the pavement a plastic delivery crate for holding bread which I obviously would not have seen if I had been on my own. I could have fallen over it, a timely reminder of the care one has to take in order to avoid accidents. Getting on the bus again presented a problem. I walked into the first step, not having raised my foot early enough, although once on the first step I negotiated the second one successfully. On reflection I concluded that this boarding of the bus problem which I experienced was due to me having too many things in my left hand and my right hand was not free for me to hold onto the bus rail. I was holding in my left hand my right hand glove, my white symbol cane (a folding cane whose purpose is to indicate that one has a visual impairment, it is not intended to be used as a mobility aid) and trying to hold Jean's arm; in my right hand I was holding my bus pass, which meant that I was really not free to hold anything or to use the cane as it should be used.

My overall impression of the day: I was very pleased with the way it had gone and I certainly had more confidence now that I had done it. But I still had the feeling when I am out that I am very, very vulnerable and it will be amazing to me if I am ever able to do that journey on my own, but I suppose that I will one day and I must work to gain the confidence to do just that.

MORE EYE PROBLEMS

During this period, would you believe, a cataract has been growing in my left eye, severely restricting the light perception/ shadow vision in that eye. On the April 22nd 1987 I was yet again admitted into the Birmingham Eye hospital, this time for the removal of this cataract which took place on the following day.

The procedure to be adopted for removal of this cataract was slightly different because remember I had a silicon oil exchange done during the last operation on the retina in this eye which meant that an implant lens was not recommended. Miss Eagling described the construction of the eye and by so doing explained that she would be removing the outer membrane which would expose the cataract crystals. These would then be flushed out leaving the back membrane in place and this membrane would then retain the silicon oil and thus maintain equal pressure on the retina.

As you can imagine the day of my admission was charged with emotion. Nicola and Jean brought me in, Nicola driving her car. We started from home at 8.45. Nicola had to be on duty at the Walsgrave hospital, Coventry, at twelve noon. We made very good time in spite of it being rush hour and arrived at the hospital at 9.45, but we didn't account however for how long it would take for me to be admitted. It took 2 hours, 2 hours which seemed more like 40 hours.

With such large organisations everything seems to take a long time and time was something which we didn't have. After blood tests and X-rays which had to be done on the ward and a lot of waiting about, I was so relieved when Jean and Nicola finally made it in a rush back to Coventry. I could tell that Jean was getting more and more agitated as the time rolled on, at the thought of Nicola having to drive out of Birmingham on her own. After the initial traumas with me saying that I didn't want to stay in this hospital I would rather be in the Nuffield, everything settled down and I was admitted on to Ward 1, the men's ward.

Dr Sheward came up to the ward and apologised for the delays and took the remainder of my particulars. I said to him, "I would have thought that by now with the number of times that I have been admitted in the last few months all my details would have been well and truly recorded by now." Nurse then came and described where I was and the layout of the ward. This time in fact it was very difficult because I had no clear picture in my mind of where I was and it wasn't possible to go down onto Ward 2, where I had always been previously, because all the single rooms were taken. As I sat on the bed feeling really sorry for myself, I then realised that there were other people in the room, Steve and James, who later on I got to know quite well. Half an hour later it was time for lunch; they obviously didn't realise at first that I was blind until they saw me feeling my way around the bed, trying to locate where things were. I then explained and we got chatting. Steve said that he would take me down to lunch and he did just that; they were both very good in fact. We had lunch, which was turkey, and during lunch we talked and they were very interested in my situation. Steve explained that he was in hospital because he had received a kick on the head while playing football on Sunday. He had been in all over the holiday weekend, but had not had any operations and it was a case of keeping him under observation.

James was also in under observation; he seemed all right and expected to be going home in a couple of days. James evidently was a painter and decorator whilst Steve said he worked in a bank as an accountant. He was hoping to take his accountancy exams later on in the month, but he was concerned because being in hospital had prevented him from doing any revision.

Late in the afternoon my luck took a turn for the better; Sister Pilcher came to me and told me that there was now a bed for me back in my old ward as Miss Eagling had released one of the patients thus freeing up a bed.

Once in my room I felt much more at ease because I knew the layout; in fact I made it down to the toilets feeling with my stick and we rearranged the room again as it had been during my previous visits. Jean and Nicola came back in the evening and brought the things that they were unable to leave earlier. I felt a lot better for seeing them in more relaxed surroundings, although Jean was very quiet. She had had a migraine during the day and she now had taken the opportunity of me being in here to have a rest, relax and recover from her ordeal; maybe I will be less impatient and more understanding of her problems after this operation.

ANOTHER OPERATION

Next day, 23rd April, was my operation day. After having two rounds of bread and butter with a little jam and a cup of tea, that was it, nil by mouth until after the operation which was timed for 2 o'clock. I found it very difficult to settle during the morning. I tried Braille which I did for the first hour or so and then I just sat, walked and stood and thought. The staff were very good; Sister Margaret came and chatted and so did the other nurses. At 1.45 I left the ward on the trolley; destination - operating theatre. We had to wait a little before they were ready. Miss Eagling came along and asked me how I was feeling, my nurse chaperon talked to me about holidays and then it was time to go into theatre.

I was wheeled into the theatre and given my injection and then just as that happened it was realised that I hadn't got my back pack on; this is a piece of equipment which monitors your heart during the operation. I remember being lifted up and the pack being fitted but before I was laid down again I was out. Next thing I remember was coming round in the operating theatre; people were talking about me, there was someone on the telephone saying, "Yes we have removed the cataract, all is OK." Then someone was speaking to me, I was trying to reply but I couldn't hear anything coming out. It was a daft situation really; it felt as if all my face was frozen and my lips wouldn't move, although I could hear myself coughing. It was a bit like being at the dentist and getting over the injection. Then I was back in my own bed lying on my right hand side, the cot rails were up and I remember nurse telling me that they were up in order that I didn't fall out of bed and bump my head on the bedside cabinet.

Later on when I was drinking a cup of Horlicks, I realised and oh what a relief it was, I felt no pain from my eye. It was heavily bandaged but I couldn't see anything; in fact there didn't seem to be as much light sensation in my right eye now. I slept on and off during the night, but I kept waking and praying to the Lord that the operation would be successful, to please let me see light.

When I awoke the next morning, Friday, I was longing for a cup of tea. I lay listening for that trolley for what seemed ages but eventually I heard it clanging along. Then nurse came in and put some drops in my right eye. I asked her when I could have the bandages off my left eye. "Later on this morning when the doctors came around," she replied. Breakfast time and the usual mix-up in the kitchens, with corn flakes instead of porridge but everyone was very kind and tolerant and nurse very helpfully buttered and jammed my bread for me.

All this time I felt myself becoming more and more worked up, only one thought was in my head: would I be able to see when the bandages came off? Whilst I was waiting I found myself constantly checking to see if I could perceive any light perception in my left eye by closing my right eye, opening my left eye and passing my hand slowly back and forth over my left eye and I did feel several times that I could see slight shadow movement through the bandages. When I looked through my right eye at the ceiling electric strip light, which was on, I could see cracks of light, rather like the veins in a leaf which confirmed that it was back to what I then called normal. My left eye, the cataract eye, was completely sealed by bandages which kept all the light away.

After what seemed to be an eternity, Sister Pilcher came in. "Right", she said, "I'm now going to do the dressing on your eye." That was quite a moment. I remember being very selfish and asking God for mercy and then came the moment. Sister started to remove the adhesive strip from the inside corner of my eye. It seemed to take ages and then suddenly it happened: I was conscious of light entering my eye.

The first thing I saw was the ceiling electric strip light, it seemed very bright and clear. Then I looked down, the television was on. I could see the square light of the screen, then I looked up and I could see Sister's back; she was wearing a blue uniform, deep blue, with white cuffs and a white hat and then just beyond her was nurse who I couldn't see so clearly but everything seemed to be so lovely. My vision obviously wasn't sharply defined, it was fuzzy, out of focus but the colours were there. I said to sister, "I can see, I can see, I can see you, you've got a dark blue dress on, I can see its white cuffs and I can see nurse on the other side of you. I can also see what you are doing with your hands, you are moving them up and down in front of me aren't you?" I held sister's hand, she squeezed it and bent over and gave me a kiss and then I remember her saying, "Oh great, that's fantastic", and I really did feel fantastic.

Sister then went away and returned a little while later with a pair of dark cataract glasses for me to wear. While she was away I said a little prayer to God, thanking him for having mercy on me. My vision was still not very clear, the eye obviously needed time to settle and the effects of the retina operations will always be there, but it was a lot, lot, lot better than before the cataract grew.

The retina seemed to have settled. I lost vision in the upper right quadrant of the eye but the lower left quadrant and left side seem to be fairly clear. This could improve in time and when I wear either a contact lens or glasses. Sister then looked into my eye with a torch and told me that it appeared lovely and clear. I felt on top of the world.

My next visitor was Dr Sheward who examined my eye. He also was pleased with what he saw and also a little emotional about me being able to see shadows. He explained that he had watched me during the previous weeks and how I was trying to cope. Not having an implant has meant that I am able to move about a little more freely, although I obviously have to be very careful in what I do, no sudden jars, jerks and not to walk into anything or anybody, no bending or doing things like that. No need to worry, I will be the most careful person on earth, now that I have been given this opportunity to see again. As I begin to settle down and get used to this vision in my left eye, I notice that the vision tails off more into the top right hand quadrant of the eye. I am told that the out of focus situation which I'm currently experiencing will be corrected/improved by wearing either a contact lens or glasses.

CHECKING WHAT SIGHT I HAVE

For the next few days I found myself being fascinated at being able to see again. I suppose to those of you reading this with normal healthy sight, the sight which I am experiencing now would seem terrible, everything being out of focus and partly missing, but to me, having just experienced no sight it was amazing and I was grateful. Referring again to my tape I note that I commented that the box which had contained my slippers was blue in colour, deep blue with a deep red framework around the edge of the lid and in the middle of the lid towards the bottom was a union jack. On the trolley at the side of my bed there was a sky blue coloured cardboard box with white tissues in it and through the open doorway I could see into the corridor and I knew that painted on the wall of the corridor was a big mural; I think it was a scene from *Jungle Book*, very appropriate as it bordered on to the children's ward. I couldn't see any detail, only just a big brown smudgy square. Something I evidently forgot to record on my tape until later was that Steve, whom I had met when I was admitted onto the other ward, visited me before I went down for my operation. He was being discharged that day and came to wish me well, as indeed I wished him well. I thought it was very nice of him.

I went on to record that following my first lunch after the operation I was able to see the colours of the food on the plate, which meant that it was much easier to find and to eat. I found the dark glasses obscured a lot of light, which was obviously good because it helped rest my eyes, but it also meant that my vision was not as clear as I believed it really was. Sister told me that the Atropine eye drops which she was putting in my eye did distort the vision anyway so I was not to worry about it. She also said the doctor had confirmed that there was 'Retina on' which meant that the retina was in place.

Quoting again directly from my tape:

> A nice surprise today, Dr King, Geoff King and his wife Monica, they were visiting Miss Eagling for Geoff's

annual check up, during which he mentioned that he knew me, upon which Miss Eagling told him that she had just removed a cataract and I was upstairs on the ward. Geoff then asked if he could come up and see me and she readily agreed, so they came up and were here talking with me for an hour I suppose. We talked about Geoff's situation, which is very similar to my own, his problems being retina detachments in both eyes. He also described his current shadow vision which seems similar to that which I am experiencing. He says that over a period of time he has settled down to the fact that he is limited to what he can do and accepts it.

Another visitor today was Pauline. She was pleased that I had my shadow vision back again; she arrived at lunch time, perfect timing as she was able to cut up my fish for me checking that there were no bones and removing the skin and would you believe it, today of all days I upset some of my bread and butter pudding into my lap; luckily no problem with my dressing, at least I don't think so as hopefully it all dropped onto the tissue on my lap but that is something which I didn't do before when I couldn't see.

Today is the second day following the operation; the eye seems to be settling down. I am still wearing my dark glasses, although I can see things faintly, that is shapes and colours; they are not in focus, in fact they appear very blurred. Nurse tells me that this blurring is caused by the Atropine eye drops which cause the pupil to dilate thus producing these distorted images and of course I have no contact lens or glasses, which I will need to correct the changes which have taken place.

These cannot be prescribed until the eye has settled down so I must be patient. The overall effect however seems to be an improvement over what I remember my very limited sight used to be following the second retina detachment operation in this eye. With regard to the focusing effect, the clarity of the upper right quadrant of my eye seems to be not as good as in the remainder of the eye, but of course that is where the fold and scars on the retina exist. Generally, though, I can see shapes and bright colours. When I look through the ward and along the corridor I can see movement which I obviously wasn't able to see before.

Today I have no visitors. Jean and Nicky came last night for a short time, Jean sounded very tired and unwell, she has had a migraine since Wednesday following the anxiety of my admission. I do hope that she will take time to relax and catch up with some rest whilst I am in this hospital, I do really worry about her.

HOME AGAIN

A few days later I recorded:

Now I am home sitting in my chair in the lounge and immediately I am aware of quite a difference in my vision. The detail of the front bow-shaped lounge window with its dividing spars is much more clearly visible. I can see the shadow of the television, the shadow of the fire and for the first time the shadow of the pictures which Jean with Nicky's assistance had fixed on the chimney breast. I tried to look at the pictures themselves but I cannot see any detail, only rough shapes of what I assume are trees. I have also noticed that I can now see the silhouette of the bannisters on the stairs, as they are painted white which makes this easier. Colours also seem to be much more prominent and helpful to navigation and orientation. On my way home from the hospital for instance, immediately I stepped out into the street I could see the shape of the pavement. When we reached Nicky's car I could see the shadowy outline of it which was a considerable improvement on what I could see before.

Looking through the bedroom window I realise I can now detect the very rough shapes of the houses opposite and if a car goes by I can see a moving blurred patch of colour cross my vision. I am now much more aware of my other eye, the right one, which is the totally blind one. This is now causing me to notice that it is producing a blind area which tends to upset my balance. To walk outside, between the side of the house and the six foot high boundary fencing is much easier by virtue of the house being painted white; this and being able to see the light contrast between the top of the fence and the sky enables me to walk straight. I have noticed that I am not feeling for the shape of the doors and the opening between the lounge and hall now, and in the garden I can see the shape of the border by the colour difference between lawn and soil and patches of colour where the flowers and shrubs are.

Having eye drops in my eyes every two hours is proving awkward for Jean as it is limiting her movements, more or less confining her to the house, so I am persevering with putting in the drops myself. To insert the drops I position the bottle containing the eye drops over my eye until I can see the shadow of the bottle and then squeeze the bottle. After some near misses and drops falling all over my face I eventually drop one in, this position I have to remember for next time; practice will make perfect.

Removal of the cataract has made quite an impact on my mobility but as far as reading is concerned there isn't any improvement. There is some light perception in the top half of my eye. Between 11 and 5 o'clock is still very fuzzy but at the extreme edges between 5 and 11 o'clock there is more detail. I am still wearing the very dark cataract glasses and have become accustomed to the shape of the pebble lens which feel like those 'bulls eye'-shaped glass panels in the windows of the old Dickensian sweet shops I remember seeing in books and on Christmas cards.

My first impressions were of the improvement in my shadow vision. This improvement made me feel much more positive; the light at this time was very bright and the weather good which all helped. The bright light helped me to pick out the colours and made the shadows more clearly defined, but there was a drawback because the shadows produced by high boundary fencing or tree branches, overhanging shop blinds and bus shelters were very dense and blocked out the shadow line which I was using as a guide. In contrast I did find the colour change line, which occurs when pavements are made up of light coloured paving slabs with an infill between paving and kerb of black tarmacadam, very useful thus making it easy to follow.

chapter five

In spite of the positive outlook now that I was becoming more mobile I was still experiencing bouts of depression, due mainly to being confined to the house and only venturing out when I have mobility lessons, go to hospital or Braille lessons. As a person who used to be very active and enjoyed walking, this is now becoming very boring and frustrating for me; it seems as though people don't want the responsibility or don't have the time to take me along, and anyway what is the point? "He can't see anything." The other day Mr Mumford, my mobility instructor, suggested to Jean because she was naturally nervous of me going out on my own, that she walk along with him, which was a little way behind me, as an observer to see just how safe I was; regrettably she declined. What everyone seems to fail to realise is that the change in environment for me at this time would be as good as a rest.

At this time a major sporting occasion occurred in Coventry. Coventry City Football Club won the F A Cup at Wembley beating Tottenham Hotspurs, the score being 3-2 to Coventry. The match was played on Saturday 16th May 1987 and as you can probably imagine the whole of Coventry was caught up in Cup fever. To remind me of my feelings on this particular day I now refer to the notes I made on my tape.

> For the first time for a little while I am feeling frustrated. I sat and listened to the match with Jean who had it on television, Nicola who is on night duties this week and has been sleeping all morning, came down and joined us for the second half. It was a very exciting game, but I found it so very frustrating not being able to see the play, but managed to cope with it and contain my feelings. What I wasn't able to cope with however was next day, the Sunday following the match, when it was

announced that the City Council were going to give a civic reception to the team to honour their achievement and the team were to drive into and around Coventry in an open topped bus in order to show off both themselves and their prize - the F A Cup. Jean, who normally has not the slightest interest in football, said she would like to go down into town and see them. I certainly would have liked to have gone along with her, to savour the atmosphere and to take some photographs. Then reality struck, who was I kidding? Of course it was pointless me going, there will be crowds everywhere, I wouldn't be able to see anything and as for taking photographs, I must really get to grips with the fact that it is an activity which is now lost to me for ever.

This has really affected me today, I am now beginning to realise just what I have lost by losing my sight. Jean went with a friend this afternoon, Sunday, leaving me alone except for little Pippa our Shetland collie. I find these days at the moment, with Nicola on night duty, very wearying. I am not really able to do very much around the house because of the noise and I'm not able to go outside because the weather at the moment is very windy and not very good, all of which is exacerbated by not being able to become involved in anything because of the delicate situation relating to my eye.

I went on to note from the comments which I had dictated following these:

Jean was becoming more and more frustrated with the situation which was not helped by her being overtired.

> I was not helping either being wrapped up in myself. I noted that I was frequently annoyed with myself, becoming very angry at the slightest little thing, having no patience and for ever feeling sorry for myself. I really did need to control my feelings, to try and accept each day as it came because at this time Eric was not an easy person to live with.

Having recovered from my cataract operation Miss Eagling suggested that she had another go at flattening the retina in my right eye by using the silicon oil exchange procedure. This operation was carried out on June 25th 1987 with, I regret, no improvement being achieved meaning that I will now remain blind, that is to say, with no light perception and now with the growth of the cataract that appears to seal its fate. It was not worth removing the cataract because all the avenues of restoring my sight had been exhausted.

I now found myself completely reliant on the residual vision in my left eye. Unfortunately I continued to suffer with problems of reoccurring inflammation and raised pressure in this eye which culminated in a sudden acute rise in pressure in early August 1989. This event caused me to be admitted into the Nuffield Hospital, Birmingham on August 7th, 1989. I underwent a glaucoma operation called an Iridectomy which involved drilling a small hole in order to allow the build-up of fluid, the cause of the pressure, to be released by allowing it to drain out into the bottom eyelid. Following this operation the pressure became much more controllable. Glaucoma eye drops were also used to assist in the control of these surges in pressure and thus help to establish a stable pressure base.

The retina in this eye was slowly detaching itself again whilst all this was going on, so a further operation was performed on the 19th November 1990 in order to try and seal this off. This operation was successful. In spite of the retina now remaining stable my vision has continued to slowly deteriorate due to the effects of glaucoma which has now set in as a result of all the pressure changes.

Another situation developed during this last period of treatment; this time it involved the membrane which was holding back the silicon oil. Remember the two membranes between which the cataract had formed? Now with the outer membrane removed along with the cataract, this inner membrane had thickened up causing a restriction in the light entering into the eye rather like another cataract. The treatment for this was, however, quite simple compared to what had gone before and involved just an afternoon visit to the clinic in the Birmingham Eye Hospital, the operation itself taking about just 5 minutes to perform.

Miss Eagling arranged that a minute hole be drilled through the centre of this membrane thus allowing in the light. The hole was to be drilled using a laser beam and its size was critical because it should not allow the silicon oil to seep out. I remember going down into the bowels of the hospital and entering a room in which I would compare the atmosphere to that of a photographic darkroom. I was guided to a chair and beckoned to sit down. In front of me resting on a table was what I took to be a slit lamp with an adjustable chin rest into which I placed my chin. A type of contact lens was then inserted into my eye using a lot of lubricant jelly in order to ease the fit; this was the most uncomfortable part of the procedure.

chapter five

The doctor then lined up what I will call his 'laser gun' with what I imagine to be a target marked on the contact lens in my eye, pin pointing where the hole should be. Having warned me what to expect and to remain perfectly still he commenced drilling. The sensations I experienced during this operation were visually seeing a turning circle of blue light in my eye, smelling a faint burning smell, but by far the greatest sensation was that of the sound the laser created in my head. It was a tearing, crackling, very loud noise which seemed to penetrate right into the skull itself. The whole procedure took only a few minutes and was completely painless and performed in very subdued lighting.

This exercise was successful. The advantage of this treatment was that almost immediately after it had been done I was aware of an improvement. To illustrate this, I will always remember standing on the platform at Birmingham New Street rail station just after having received this laser treatment, waiting with Jean for the train to take us back to Coventry. The Intercity train came in and as it approached and passed us I became very aware of the bright yellow front of the engine. It is interesting how particular things stand out in one's memory and that is certainly one of them.

From then on Miss Eagling advised me to never lie flat on my back but to always lie on my side. The reason was that lying on my back would cause the oil to rise to the top of the eye and thus run the risk of it seeping out through the hole which had been drilled.

You never miss a thing until it's not available or you are not allowed to do it any more. I now realise how often I used to lie on my back and how much I enjoyed doing it. Now that I have accepted it, it doesn't bother me too much as I can still lie on my stomach, no problems. I do have to remember however, should I go into hospital or receive treatment to any other portion of my body, which has happened in amongst all these goings on, I have to advise whoever it may concern of my problem in order that they do not allow me to be laid flat on my back, for example in the operating theatre.

Life gets complicated doesn't it? In spite of all the knowledge and skills that have been exercised on my behalf in order to restore my sight, I am now totally blind with no light perception. I have been very fortunate in having Miss Eagling, one of the country's leading specialists in the retina field, together with very dedicated nursing staff, of whom there are far too many to mention by name, looking after me throughout these years of treatment. The opportunities that they have created in order for me to participate in frank discussions about my situation, the patience, caring and the time spent in observing my progress, not to mention the support shown in so many different ways to both myself and my family has really been appreciated and has played a major part in motivating me to reach my current stage of development. No one could have worked harder than Miss Eagling and it must have been very frustrating for her to have every attempt to restore my sight thwarted. Right throughout the series of operations she has been so patient, so understanding and caring. Each step along the way has been discussed and in quite a lot of detail which gave me confidence; I knew exactly what was happening and what the chances of success were.

So, all the work, suffering and pain have been to no avail? Or has it? People very often say to me, "Who do you blame for all that has happened?" I can honestly say that I blame no one.

chapter five

Now many years on from that fateful day I am blind. Was there a purpose behind it I often ask myself? On reflection, as time moves on, I feel more and more convinced that perhaps there was. God has a plan for each and every one of us. Sometimes people become aware of this; for example how often have you heard someone explain that they felt a calling to live their life in a certain way; or to work in religious orders.

When I look back on the work in which I used to be involved, prior to the commencement of my eye problems, I realise that the knowledge and expertise which I acquired during this time are now helping me to fulfil this new role in which I find myself. It's a role in which I have no written plan to guide me. I don't plan things, they just happen. And so one thing leads to another and so on, as you will gather, from reading the developments that have occurred which I describe in detail as you read on through this book.

I have already indicated that in my business career everything was planned. I used many tools and acquired skills to achieve results, so it is interesting now to find that I am again using those same skills to achieve results of a different kind in the work in which I am now involved. An example of this is the use of the skills I learnt from having to give lectures and product presentations to both potential and existing customers, something in which I gained confidence and which I enjoyed. One of the activities in which I now find myself is giving talks to all sorts of groups of children and adults about my own experiences in relation to becoming blind and I now find that I have been given the opportunity of using those same skills to continue doing something which I enjoy, which is positive and is hopefully helping to raise public awareness and help others.

I leave it to you, the reader, to judge for yourself. For me, as time progresses, I become more firmly convinced that there is a pattern emerging which links all the various facets of my life together for some purpose of which I am not yet aware, the thought of this, however, is helping me to let things just happen. My experiences during this part of my life have served to heighten my awareness and dependence upon our Lord and Saviour. I say my Saviour for that is what he has proved to be.

I certainly believe in the power of prayer. As you will have gathered I have spent a lot of time praying, yes selfishly for myself and for my family. There have been certain times when I was in hospital that suddenly, out of the blue, I have experienced a warm, uplifting feeling of peace, which upon reflection the only explanation for which has been the power of prayer, other people's prayers, in which I have figured. I reach this conclusion as I discovered that the times roughly coincided with the times that various prayer groups and services have been held back in my local church.

I have also been fortunate to sometimes experience a special feeling of peace when being near to God in his house. This happened during a brief visit to the Nun's private chapel at Our Lady of Walsingham's shrine. I cannot explain this feeling, except that I would like to experience it again. I also come much closer to God when I take Holy Communion, an act which has become more meaningful for me during this period.

CHAPTER 6

I LEARN TO LIVE AGAIN

It was a Sunday evening and I was in the Birmingham Eye Hospital and Miss Eagling had come in to see me and check how my eye was recovering after the latest operation. We went through the normal examination routine under the slit lamp after which she asked me to ease back and said "I suggest we register you blind." It was silly really because I knew I couldn't see, but that statement devastated me. I suddenly realised my name was going to be written on a piece of paper, a legal document and that sounded so very final.

I returned to my bed and lay down; all night I tossed and turned and needless to say I didn't get any sleep. I kept thinking of Jean and Nicola. I wouldn't see their faces and endearing ways again and the pain of this realisation hurt deeply and was something that I could not even begin to comprehend, the pain those thoughts provoked hurt so much. Neither would I again see our dog Pippa, with her loving welcomes and wagging tail and that special smile which was now lost to me for ever.

I am a fiercely independent person, my various professional occupations supported this and I just couldn't bear the thought of being dependent upon someone, for something, for the rest of my life. So the questions continued to race through my mind: how can I? How could you? How can I? How can I?

A HELPING HAND

Next morning a lady appeared at my bedside. She was Mrs Warmsley and she was the social service worker based in the hospital and trained to help people with a visual disability, particularly people in trauma to rehabilitate. She drew up a chair and sat down at my bedside, took my hand in hers, and said, "OK let's have all those questions that have been pouring through your head during the night out into the open and we'll see if we can find some positive answers to them."

She was marvellous and seemed to immediately give me the confidence to talk and oh how I needed to talk. So out poured all those thoughts and questions that had been racing around in my head. My first question, how can I communicate? I can't write or read and if there is to be a future I need to be able to communicate.

"Yes you can write," Mrs Warmsley advised and seeing the obvious disbelief on my face and guessing correctly my instant thoughts, "What is this woman talking about, how can I possibly write I cannot see, doesn't she understand that?" She repeated, "Oh yes you can write and I will show you how." She then produced a writing frame, which I can only describe as a kind of picture frame complete with picture and backing but instead of a picture, substitute a sheet of writing paper which can be easily inserted and removed from inside the frame; secure a louvre type blind, fixed along the bottom width of the picture frame so that when it is fully extended it covers the writing paper inside the frame.

To begin writing take a pencil or pen; feel for the writing point with your finger in order that you have the pencil positioned correctly and turn down the first slat of the louvre. This then exposes a clean rectangular strip of writing paper on which to write. Feel for the left hand edge of the exposed writing paper and begin to write, remembering to put a finger of your non-writing hand on the end of the last word written in order that you do not start your next word on top of the one just written. When the first line of writing has been completed, turn down the next slat thus exposing another clean rectangle of paper and so the process is repeated, each time the slat serving as a writing guide. Well I persevered with my practise writing, but the only problem was I could not, of course, see what I was writing and had no idea how successful my efforts were, but it kept me occupied and at that time it was very important for me to be occupied.

Imagine the boost to my confidence then when Nicola came to visit me with Jean and after a little while suddenly asked, "Dad have you been writing? No, you couldn't have because you can't see, but I've been reading a note on the top of your locker and I have a feeling that you had written it. On the other hand, it couldn't be you because no one could read your writing when you could see." I smiled, remembering that was true and even I couldn't read my own writing; you know how it is, your brain is racing ahead and your poor old fingers can't keep up, with the result that the standard of writing is terrible. My writing now, however, is produced much more slowly as I picture the words and letters in my mind as I write them which results in, hopefully, well formed and spaced letters and consequently they are able to be read and understood. That little exercise together with Nicola's ability to read my note gave me an awful lot of confidence and that was what I was desperately in need of.

"Do you play dominoes?" asked Mrs Warmsley the next morning. "I expect you are getting a little tired of all that writing aren't you? Well I've brought you a set of dominoes to play with." When I opened the box I could feel that these dominoes were rather different from those which I had previously played with. The markings on these dominoes were raised rather like little pimples, whereas those I had previously played with had had dished markings like little saucers. The purpose of these raised markings was to provide a positive tactile indication of each domino's marking.

Again I practised playing with the dominoes and soon became quite confident. I even asked the nurses if they would play a game with me. Mrs Warmsley's next little surprise was a game of *Mastermind*, not the usual one however which I had previously played. In this game the pegs with the flat circular coloured disc tops, you know the ones, those which you hide behind the screen in colour combinations of your choice, had been modified. The objective of those playing this game was to work out the colour combination which has been selected by the code maker and hidden behind the screen. Obviously colours were of little use to people who couldn't see them, so this game differed in that instead of the pegs having flat coloured tops the colours had been replaced with narrow pins projecting from off the peg's flat top. I quickly realised that these pins, or needles as I preferred to call them as they were quite sharp, appeared in different combinations similar to the pimples on the dominoes or the dots on a games dice. I found these pins very difficult to feel, as my finger tips were not sensitive enough. In fact at first I couldn't feel the different points and became very frustrated, but I persevered and eventually with lots of practice I began to succeed, being encouraged by the nurses who grabbed the odd spare few minutes to play with me.

Next to arrive on my locker was a wooden cube. It was split into three parallel planes which revolved independently to each other, each of the four sides in each section having brass cup headed nails driven into them. By revolving the three different sections, one could produce different combinations of nail heads and again combination patterns such as found on the dominoes and *Mastermind* pegs could be produced. Mrs Warmsley was clever, and very understanding of the situation, for what she had been doing was keeping me occupied, giving me positive things to do and by these means introducing me to the idea of using my fingers to replace my eyes in a tactile way and at the same time building my confidence.

Realising that I seemed to be mastering these various tactile patterns Mrs Warmsley asked me one morning, "Do you realise what we have been building up to?" I exclaimed that I had no idea. "Well you have been learning to read with your fingers the basic cell of Braille". Braille is a method using embossed dots on paper which blind people are able to feel with their fingers and thus convert sighted text into an accessible format.

Later on after the operation traumas and things settled down a little I went on to learn Braille. It took me about twelve months to grasp the basics and start reading, which I then followed up by learning to type. I reflected on the use of this Braille as it was certainly an aid to communication providing that everyone understood it. Sadly however only about 5% of all visually impaired people are motivated to learn and use it.

As most sighted people do not read Braille I needed to find a better system of communication. I remembered my small pocket tape recorder that I used in my work; in fact it became an inseparable part of me when I was out of my office, especially on overseas visits. I used it for dictating reports, letters and memos, sending the tapes back to my secretary for action back home. I thought to myself, I could use that little pocket tape recorder to help me communicate with other people in the same way as I used it to communicate with my secretary.

I could record messages on audio cassette which could be letters which could be sent through the post, replies could be returned to me using the same method especially if I used standard cassettes which the majority of people use. One other plus point here which I was to discover later was that registered blind people are allowed to send and receive information in Braille and on audio cassette through the post free, with no postal charges providing the envelope or special wallet can be easily opened for examination by postal staff. The use of audio cassettes in this way means that all kinds of information could be stored and communicated such as my friends' addresses, telephone numbers, telephone messages, even my shopping list and later on if a situation arose where a friend called unexpectedly and invited me out for a drive and Jean was out I could leave a message for her on tape in a place where, upon returning home she would find it. She could play it back and thus receive the message and not worry about me.

I was beginning to feel better already and to find solutions for myself and that's exactly what Mrs Warmsley was doing. She was encouraging me to think positively, by keeping me active and occupied and achieving this, she was helping me to build confidence in both myself and the future.

"This is all very fine but how am I going to be able to feed myself? For instance I can't see the food on my plate. Is it easier to use a spoon to eat with instead of a knife?" "Why on earth should you do that? You don't want to draw attention to yourself do you?" replied Mrs Warmsley. "When your situation has settled a little you will probably go out to a café or restaurant for a meal or go visiting friends. I wouldn't suggest you draw attention to yourself by being different and that's what you would be doing. People, and particularly children, would prod each other and point to you asking, "What's the matter with that man? Look, he's using a spoon instead of a knife", and you don't want that to happen do you? So just get on with it and learn to use your cutlery just the same as you used to do." And I did.

What Mrs Warmsley did do, however, was to explain to me how I could identify where and what the food was on my plate. This is done by asking the person who serves you with your food to identify where it is on your plate by using the clock method. By that I mean, that you both should imagine the plate to be the face of a clock with clear hour markings around its perimeter. When the plate containing the food has been placed in front of you the sighted person should describe what food is on the plate and where it is in relation to the hour marking. For example, "You have potatoes between 12 o'clock and 3 o'clock, cabbage between 3 o'clock and 6 o'clock, roast beef between 6 o'clock and 9 o'clock and if you are lucky Yorkshire pudding between 9 o'clock and 12 o'clock. Simple isn't it?" she added.

chapter six

It is, except for one little difficulty and this happens to all of us when we eat our food, be we visually impaired or not. One of my eating habits was to put a selection of different foods and tastes on my fork at the same time. This now presents difficulties so I tend to load the fork with only one item of food at a time. The problem occurs however when it is being transported to your mouth as sometimes before it reaches your mouth it falls off the fork, but it doesn't fall back to where it came from with the result that towards the end of the meal you are experiencing a type of taste lucky dip.

As time has passed my eating experiences have reinforced my belief that one's sense of taste is very much determined by one's sight. One Sunday lunch the family were all enjoying the fruit pie and custard which Jean had prepared, when I casually remarked that I hadn't realised that Jean had been baking that morning but it was a pleasant surprise because I was really enjoying the apple pie. There was no reply so I repeated myself, still no reply. There was a long pause before Nicola enquired, "Apple pie?" "Yes," I said, "It's really nice." Another long pause before Nicola again enquired "Are you really sure that it's apple pie?" I tasted it and smelt it again, "Yes I am," I confirmed. "It's not, you know," she said "It's cherry pie," and sure enough it was cherry pie.

On another occasion we were having afternoon tea whilst watching television, when I remarked that I was enjoying the cheese sandwiches which Jean had made, although I couldn't quite remember having had that particular kind of cheese before. When I asked what kind it was, she rather indignantly retorted: "Cheese?! I'll have you know it's turkey." So much for my taste buds.

Thinking of food my mind began to race ahead. How was I going to cope with food preparation? Being dependent upon someone to even pour a drink for me was certainly not my style and besides which it was going to be difficult for those around me. Jean would have no life of her own if she had constantly to be at my beck and call.

"There is no reason why after advice and some practical training you shouldn't prepare your own food," advised Mrs Warmsley. "For instance, to pour yourself a drink without spilling it or scalding your finger all you need is a simple little device called a level indicator", whereupon she produced one for me to examine. I ran my fingers over it feeling the circular plastic housing which contained the batteries, little ones of the type used in hearing aids and cameras. The housing measured 1.5 inches diameter x 0.75 inches deep approximately and resembled something like the feel of a 10 foot flexible tape measure case which I frequently used around the house when attending to the DIY jobs. As my fingers explored further, that opinion was confirmed because where I would expect the tape to project from the case, 2 plastic covered wires projected forming a hook thus enabling the device to hang onto the lip of a cup or glass so that the two wire probes could project down into the cup.

With the device placed on the lip of the cup one poured a drink in the normal manner. When the hot tea or cold milk level reaches the tips of the probes it has the effect of closing an electrical circuit and causing a buzzer to sound in the housing which indicates the cup is full and you stop pouring. Further enhancements have been made to enable the device to indicate milk level or for those who are accustomed to taking stronger medicine, gin perhaps? It also incorporates a vibratory motion which assists people who are both hard of hearing and blind. It simply is not possible to calculate the effect this simple, inexpensive little device has had on people like myself. It has brought so much independence and peace of mind and has proved to be such an important step in that confidence-building exercise.

"Now I can pour myself a drink without flooding the room or scalding my finger, but what if I wanted to prepare a snack for myself? Something like beans on toast, for instance?" "No problem", came the reply. "First let's get the beans warming. Take the tin of beans and open the tin using a safety can opener, the kind which when you open the handle sits on the top of the tin locating itself on the rim; upon closing the handle punctures the tin just below the rim on the side. Turning the opener handle then moves the opener around the tin at the same time cutting through it and bevelling the cut edges in order that they do not present sharp edges. Feel for the saucepan and once you have located it, empty the beans into it and transfer to the cooking hob."

In my case it is a gas hob. Mrs Warmsley told me that to feel around the base of the saucepan to ensure that it is located centrally on the burner and then ignite the gas. Most gas appliances these days have automatic ignition, which I would say is a must in terms of safety. Having ignited the gas listen for the sizzling noise which the beans make when they are warming. Once you hear it, time them based on your experience obtained by trial and error. Adjustment to the degree of heat provided by the burner to the underside of the saucepan may be made by adjusting the control knob in the normal way but with one exception, a blind person obviously cannot see the knob setting or the height of the burner flame, so a tactile form of identification is required. Tactile marking of appliance controls can be done in many ways such as in Braille or by using Bump ons, which are small plastic or rubber knobs of various sizes which can be stuck on as required. Assistance in the marking of appliances may be obtained from several sources such as your local social services rehabilitation officer, your local Society for the Blind or their Resource Centre, the local customer care or service representative of both British Gas or the local Electricity Board. When buying new appliances some manufacturers will provide the appliance with the controls already marked for you.

Subsequently my experience has proved that British Gas provide an excellent service to people with sight difficulties, they produce both general, safety and recipe information on audio cassette; no charge is made for providing this service.

"Whilst the beans are warming we can turn our attention to the toast", continued Mrs Warmsley. "Take a slice of bread, I think it's always better to buy and use ready sliced bread, it's more convenient and the slices are of uniform thickness. If you are using the grill, put your slice onto the toast rack and ignite the grill; you can tell when it's on as you will hear the noise and can feel the heat; to produce toast to your own individual liking, you will learn from experience the feel of the surface of the bread with your fingers. The same technique applies when you use an automatic toaster but this has the advantage that when you have recognised the texture of the toast which is to your liking you can set the timer control position to suit. Don't worry if you burn your toast as you will smell it by which time it will be too late so just open the door or window and give the birds a treat."

chapter six

Then I had a sudden thought: "Hang on," I exclaimed. "You said open a can of beans but how am I going to find which can contains the beans when I open the cupboard door? I might pick up a tin of rice pudding and I don't think I like rice pudding on toast." Now, when I talk to children I describe this experience by asking them to imagine that when they open the cupboard door all the labels on the tins are missing, how would they find the tin which contains the beans? Again Mrs Warmsley comes to the rescue: "Quite simple, you use a metallic dymo strip tape label which has a magnetic backing. You write beans on the label in Braille and put it onto the tin and then you are able to identify it by reading the label with your finger. An alternative, especially for those people who are not able to read Braille is to use magnetic shapes." "What are those?" I enquired. "Have you not seen children playing with those little plastic figures of Walt Disney characters? They have magnetic backing strips and children love to play with them sticking them to fridge doors." "Yes I have," I confirmed. "Well all you have to do is to acquire a supply of these characters. You will find that they are very tactile and can therefore be very easily recognised and stick them onto the tins choosing a certain character for each different product."

Great, I thought, I like beans so there will be several tins of these in my cupboard and one of my favourite characters is Donald Duck so I will mark my tins of beans with Donald Duck. Well another problem solved, but what a surprise for anyone opening my cupboard door and finding all these little characters looking at them.

Well by this time this encouragement in positive thinking was beginning to have an effect. I was starting to believe that perhaps there were ways of living with this blindness; in any case I had no choice, so get on with it Eric.

My thoughts were now beginning to sort themselves out into sequences:
I have been shown how to communicate
How to feed myself
How to prepare simple little snacks for myself

This was all very fine but I anticipate that I will eventually be getting out and about and there's a problem. "When I dress myself how do I know which clothes I am putting on and more important how can I ensure that when I do go out, I don't look like a Harlequin character causing everyone to stop and stare at me and laugh because I am wearing clothes which obviously don't match."

This time Mrs Warmsley brought me a small packet of buttons and when I felt them they were all in different shapes diamonds, daisy, triangular, stars, octagonal and squares with each shape a specific colour. "The method to be adopted when using these buttons, when followed correctly, will ensure that all your clothes match and removes the possibility of you becoming the subject of ridicule," reassured Mrs. Warmsley. "Choose a button shape that you find easy to identify and use that for your favourite or most common colour clothes. What you do is to sew this shaped button on all those garments which are of that colour and their coordinates. Sew it on the tail of a shirt, the waistband inside your trousers, the label in a sweater, on the inside pocket of your suit or sports jacket, the inside top of your socks and so on. To use this identification system all you do is to ensure that when you dress, all the garments you put on all have the same matching shaped buttons. A further advantage for those people who are partially sighted, the buttons all having a specific colour for each shape makes identification that much easier."

So now I can feel easier in my mind knowing that I am in control of the clothes I wear and the chances of me putting on a white sock with a black sock, purple trousers with a green shirt and jacket are minimal. Of course as time progressed I realised that it would be advisable to restrict my wardrobe to only one or two main colours and having all my clothes in these or their coordinates, would help make life much simpler. At present however, I cannot afford to discard those clothes that don't fit into these categories. My choice of clothes is also affected as I will have to be much more practical in my choice and they will have to be longer lasting and universal. I just said 'My choice'; in practice I really don't have a choice, particularly in terms of appearance and that hurts. I am going to be dependent upon someone else telling me if my clothes suit me or not. In other words I am not going to be me any more in terms of appearance but someone else's person.

Now that I can dress myself I shall want to visit the shops, to make purchases. I will have to travel on the buses, trains and taxis, all of which require money, so how do I cope with this? "The best advice I can give you,", said Mrs Warmsley, "is to practise handling the coins, feeling them in terms of size, shape and weight. Feel the edges: are they smooth as in the case of the copper coins, 1p and 2p, or are they milled like the 5 and 10p silver coins?"

Later after I had left hospital and was at home with time on my hands I asked Jean to visit the bank and obtain £5 in assorted small change. With this I then played those games with the family; you know the kind, playing post offices and shops, like I did as a small boy, buying and selling but this time using real money, giving and receiving change. I could soon tell the differences; for example, the 50p coin is easy to detect due to both its size and shape and the long flat sides are a big help in identifying it. This is in sharp contrast to the 20p coin which is the same shape but much smaller. The £1 coin was also quite easy to identify as it's heavy, chunky and has milled edges also.

I was advised to be careful with bank notes as it is very easy when under pressure to make a mistake. For instance when you are in a queue of people at the check-out in the supermarket and the assistant is waiting there with her hand out. Bank notes are identified by their different widths and for those who are partially sighted, by colour. I was given a useful little pocket gauge; it felt and probably looked rather like a flight of steps which projected above a rectangular piece of plastic which had a groove running along its bottom edge parallel to the projecting steps. To use this gauge you place the bank note in the groove and read off with your finger the step with which the opposite (top) edge of the note aligns. It is advisable for both security and peace of mind to carry only one denomination of bank note and £5 is recommended as it is the lowest value note in circulation at the present time. If you carry only one denomination of bank note you are always sure that when you give a note for a purchase you know its value. Likewise when you receive money which includes bank notes always insist that the bank notes are £5 ones.

It is important to be seen to be confident when handling money, as it dissuades the thief who doesn't miss an opportunity to short change, who may think that as you are blind you are easy pickings. The ability to handle money in a competent manner is also a big booster to one's own confidence. My confidence was also boosted when, much later on, some friends of mine, who used to do voluntary work raising funds for Guide Dogs. were having a flag day in the local town of Kenilworth. They asked me if I would like to go along and help them count the money collected in the collecting boxes. I agreed and after helping to count around £350 in assorted small change I reckoned that I could confidently handle money.

A further big boost to one's confidence and independence is to be able to sign one's own signature. Signing your signature means that you are once again in charge of your own affairs and there is really no need for someone else to have to sign on your behalf. Another exercise in keeping me occupied and thinking positive was practising writing my signature, using a template made from a rectangular piece of plastic, white one side and on the other side black thus providing varying contrasts for those people who are partially sighted. This rectangular plastic sheet had a rectangular slot cut in it which acted as a template in which one could sign one's name.

Other templates are readily available from Social Services and the banks which make signing cheque or benefit books so easy.

Bank cheques can be written using a template, this time with a down-standing flange which locates it very positively into the cheque book; this template has slots cut into it which align with the areas on the cheque which have to be completed. To help remind the memory of what is required to be written in the individual slot, the instruction is embossed in Braille on the template, this means a little more practice but think of the independence it brings; you could now shop from your own home. Like pouring a cup of tea having control over your own finances provides a great sense of achievement and a big step up the ladder to independence.

During my numerous periods of residence in hospital receiving treatment it was very important that I remained mobile; lying in bed all the time was not good for the rest of my body and worse still for me psychologically. Sister Margaret Perry or Mrs. Warmsley, I cannot remember which, taught me that from now on, whenever I was walking about, for my own safety, I must remember to adopt a technique which involved crossing my right arm across my chest parallel to the floor and projecting about one foot from my body. In this way one would hit any obstructions immediately in front in the line of route with one's forearm and thus prevent the rest of the body making contact, particularly the head which at this time was very vulnerable. At a later stage I was given a white symbol cane with which I could sweep the floor checking for any obstructions which may be in my path.

During these short walkabouts around the ward and adjoining corridor I found myself, after each operation, constantly checking the light perception/vision in my eyes. I remember that one seemingly reliable check was to look at the neon strip lighting in the ceiling, closing or covering one eye alternately to do so. Regardless of the fact that they were all I could see, they proved a good gauge because I was able to see the parts that were missing. These related to those areas of my retina not functioning, problems of fuzzy images could be seen and monitored, as could also the colour of the light. My life became a victim to this constantly checking syndrome. All the time I found myself checking my vision, had it improved or had it deteriorated, which in turn fuelled the anxiety and trauma I was experiencing. Not only was I peering at the strip lights but trying to read notices on doors with my nose only inches from them and I shall always remember a floor to ceiling mural painted in bold colours of a scene from *Jungle Book* in the children's ward, now this really was a good test. So my hopes for recovery rocketed one minute, only to be plummeted into the depths of despair the next, depending upon the results of my rather crude testing technique.

It was in these early days of constant anxiety and spells of depression that I realised that if I was to come through this retaining some measure of independence and keeping to a minimum the problems the imposition that my blindness was going to be on the family, then I needed to be occupied both physically and mentally. Mrs Warmsley had exactly the right idea when she started me playing dominoes. I remember when I was at home recovering from either the second or third operations, the time was dragging, I needed to be occupied and feel useful, so I asked around, had any of my friends any ideas and sure enough someone suggested I stuff soft toys, so I stuffed soft toys. Miss Barnacle, a lady who lived quite close to us, spent her spare time making soft toys which were sold at fetes and bazaars in order to raise money for charities such as the Children's Hospital and Riding for the Disabled. She used to deliver a large sack of cotton wool type material used for the stuffing and a selection of arms, legs and bodies which she had cut out and sewn together which I then used to stuff with the aid of a knitting needle packing the material in very firmly.

CHAPTER 7

Mobility, the Long Cane version

Although I had become accustomed to walking about around the ward area all my walking had been done on the same level so what I was about to experience came as a great shock. Not the kind of feeling I wish to experience again, although to be fair Sister Margaret had warned me to be careful when negotiating stairs and steps for the first time.

This experience occurred the first time that I left the Birmingham Eye Hospital after being registered blind. Jean and Nicola had come to collect me and take me home in Nicola's car. Previously I had always travelled up and down the building in the lift, and I had not really used the stairs at all. This time I went down in the lift to the ground floor, I then walked through the main reception area out to the street. Just before the street however there were three steps to negotiate.

As I approached the first step Nicola directed me, telling me to stop when I arrived at the start of the first one. I took hold of the handrail which was situated on my right hand side and then very gingerly put my foot down, feeling for the second step. Oh boy! What an experience! It was just as though I was putting my foot down into the bowels of the earth. I thought I was at least going to end up in Australia and the feeling was ever so strange and horrible. Then came the second step and the same feeling and then the third step and out into the street with just a shallow step onto the street level.

Another frightening experience; I was suddenly out into the street and all around me there was noise. It sounded terrific: cars starting, lorries turning, buses stopping with their brakes squealing, footsteps, people hurrying past, people shouting, the noise made by construction work going on at nearby Snow Hill rail station. What made it so frightening was the fact that I could not see anything except light. I couldn't see any shapes, no shadows, nothing.

I grabbed hold of both Jean's and Nicola's arms and held on very firmly. We only had to walk a short distance around the corner to the car but it seemed like a marathon and by the time I got to the car I was shaking like a jelly. Once inside the car I felt safe and secure again and started to relax and off home we sped. Nicola drove very carefully, obviously being very mindful of how I was feeling; for my part I just kept my eyes tightly closed all the way.

When I arrived home it was a lovely feeling to be back inside the safety of my house and the feeling of security which it gave me. I knew this environment. Nothing had been moved in the house during my absence, I knew where everything was, especially the chairs and tables. Little Pippa came to greet me, I felt her wagging her tail and brushing against my legs, Sadly I couldn't see her curling her lips in that special greeting smile, but I bet that's what she was doing.

Following this experience I certainly didn't leave the house to go out on my own. I did gain a little confidence by going out with Jean, but only when I had to, to keep hospital and other appointments. I remember one occasion when I was invited to sit in during a volunteers' committee meeting at the Guide Dog Training Centre in Leamington. This was because I had become bored with my own company and so I had approached them to see if there was anything that I could do to help. They had suggested that bearing my background in mind that I might like to consider becoming a speaker at their visitors' afternoons.

Hazel, wife of the centre's appeal manager, collected us from home in a car and took us to the Guide Dog training centre. After the meeting we made our own way home. Guiding me in a new environment was another new experience for Jean as she had not received any information or training on how to do this; it proved to be a very daunting task. I remembered from my sighted days the route back into Leamington from the training centre and all went well until we entered the town. Jean had difficulty in coping with me, the shopping and the amount of people around, particularly in large stores such as Marks and Spencers, so we bought what we had to and made a dash for the bus stop and home. These experiences tend to shake my confidence in getting around in town and in stores I tend to get parked by the empty shopping trolleys, whilst the shopping is done; still I knew we must persevere.

As time went by I found myself growing more and more eager to receive my mobility lessons because I knew that the major key to my independence was being mobile, to be able to go out and about, to do my own shopping and visit friends as you do when you are sighted. I just couldn't wait to start learning how to do this and grew very impatient.

Then it happened. I note from my tape the following record:

> David Mumford, the Social Services Manager in charge of services for the blind in Coventry, who is also a mobility officer, visited me today and spent an hour or so with me, talking about making arrangements for getting me mobile again, teaching me the use of the long cane for getting about the area. I found the visit useful, positive and encouraging for me. Later however I realise that Jean feels that she is being left out of this support package and she is having to cope with the increased responsibilities as best she can. I on the other hand am receiving quite a lot of help from people which seems unfair. This situation is getting Jean down and is causing problems between us, which at this time I don't know how to cope with.

On the March 25th 1987 David Mumford came to take me out on my first mobility lesson. He collected me in his car and took me to the Memorial Park which is situated quite close to where we live. I made the following notes on my tape concerning this day.

> Today was fantastic: it was the first time that I've been able to walk at my own pace since becoming blind and I thoroughly enjoyed it. The technique was surprising. I walked from the car park to the junction of the Kenilworth and Leamington roads following the path inside the park without any stick or other aid. I was able to do this by following David's voice as he was walking backwards in front of me. It really was quite an exhilarating experience to be free and walking and one which I will never forget. I remember thinking to myself that it must have been quite amusing for anyone watching us during that first walk because, as I recall it,

we started off with me being led by David from his car to the footpath and then being placed in the middle of that path in preparation for the walk.

David then explained where we were going to walk and how. He said, "Now I am going to walk in front of you and you're going to walk towards me following my voice and to make this easier for you I will be walking backwards; you won't be using a stick, neither will you be holding me." Obviously I was nervous at first and it must have showed as after all this was the first time that I had tried to walk like this since it all happened nearly two years ago. My first steps were hesitant and difficult, not being able to see what was around me and the concentration needed to follow David's voice was unnerving.

I heard him saying "Come on, I can't really believe that this is your normal walking pace, come on! Step out and let's see what you can really do." "Well no," I said "it isn't," and at that I thought to myself, OK, what have I got to lose? David's in front of me, facing me and walking backwards, he can see me and won't let me come to any harm, so I did begin then to step out. As we were walking I could hear and was conscious of people who were out walking and exercising their dogs in the park passing by or standing on the grass on the edges of the path, keeping out of our way and giving us plenty of room. At one point I remember suggesting to David that it might be a good idea if he were to have fitted to his rear two flashing lights, one on the back of his head and the other on his back side, in order to warn oncoming pedestrians of our approach!

> The second walk was also positive and on this one I graduated to a long cane which was thicker and longer than the one I had previously been using which was evidently called a symbol cane because, as its name suggests it was really an identification to tell people the holder was blind. On the second and third walks in the park I was able to identify the shelter, situated by the side of the path, by listening for the echo of my cane from off its inside walls as I walked past.

So impressed and confident was I after these walks that I volunteered to accompany Nicola when she went to collect her car following its service at the garage and yes, you've guessed it, our route took us through the park. As I walked, I did my best to copy the exercise which I had carried out in the morning. Again it was a pleasant experience, this time with Nicola walking on my left hand side, with me finding my route in the middle of the path, using the position of her voice as a guide.

I appeared to be able to negotiate the kerbs alright without being told where they were, my positioning along the route also seemed to be fairly well defined. I felt very confident but I hope not too confident. I note from my tape that I made the following comment:

> Today's experience using the long cane seems to indicate that it may be better to have a replaceable ball on the end rather than the current needle point which seems to dig into the path and is quickly worn away.

I went on to say that after a further three lessons in the park, I felt that I was making progress, or at least I was still feeling quite confident, I was now able to distinguish where the garage and the covered seating area were located by using the echo sounds.

Operation of the long cane was becoming easier the more I practised with it. I needed to develop a smooth rhythm sweeping from right to left and left to right as I walked. I was also finding the kerb much easier now using the cane in this manner because I now found that as I approached the kerb, I could feel my cane slip down from off the pavement level down into the gutter, and as I realised that my next stride brought my foot up to the kerb edge whereupon I stopped.

When it was felt that I had gained sufficient confidence and skill to leave the park and venture out into the streets I found that my first difficulty was one of coping with uneven pavement slabs; the cane tip catches the upstanding edge of the slab and of course it stops the movement of the cane forwards whereupon one is caused to walk into the handle. Most times it caught me in the side of the body or lower abdomen and I can tell you it hurts.

The sounds which I could hear around me became more important as aids to navigation. For instance when approaching a major road, the noise created by the traffic using it acts as a warning. Also when walking along a busy road the noise of the traffic going past enables one to walk parallel to the traffic flow. I remember that during this first part of my mobility training we experienced the foulest of weather with gale force winds and heavy rain and I was for ever getting a soaking. One thing which I quickly noticed during these variations in the weather was that the sounds around me also varied with the changing weather and I therefore needed to be aware of this and be prepared to make any necessary allowances when out.

Knowing when to turn a corner at the junction of two roads was a particular challenge especially when using the traffic noise as an aid to navigation.

An exercise which David had me doing was to walk along in the gutter tapping the side of the kerb with my long cane and by doing so using the kerb as a guide. He explained that there would probably be many instances when I would have to do this in order to manoeuvre around obstacles. I became aware of the problems which a camber on a drive or footpath can cause; many times I was diverted off my stride and line of travel by one of these. I remember David having a good laugh at my expense on one such occasion. Evidently I had been walking along very well keeping a reasonable line along the near middle of the footpath when I encountered a wide driveway which had been recently tarmaced and which stretched out to meet the kerb. There was quite a sharp camber on this drive which led me off the path and to follow up the drive, whereupon my cane moving from left to right had started to behead some daffodils which were growing along the edge of the drive; all this was watched by a startled lady in the house who just couldn't believe what was happening and more to the point how she could stop me. Fortunately I was quickly rescued by David who apologised on my behalf.

Walking along a narrow footpath, 2 foot, 6 inches wide, for the first time also became quite a challenge; it was like I imagine walking along a tight rope would be, but I managed it successfully. Crossing minor roads at their junction with a major road demands a new technique for those who are visually impaired. No longer should one cross the minor road following the line of route being taken when one is walking on the pavement parallel to the major road. Crossing the road in the normal sighted person's way makes one vulnerable to making the crossing at an oblique angle thus running the risk of walking out into the major road and maybe even along it with disastrous results; indenting, as we call it, down the minor road takes into account any such mistake by keeping you still within the minor road and therefore safe. Crossing roads by this method seems so long-winded that one is tempted to ignore the training until one realises that it incorporates an important safety feature.

Another thing I found quite amazing, was when I was walking along keeping in the middle of the pavement with traffic approaching from behind. Whenever I turned to face this traffic to hear better, I found that I veered off my course towards this traffic, it seemed to have some pulling power, something which I didn't appreciate when I was sighted.

The importance of using the cane correctly was brought home to me on one occasion. I had become confused whilst trying to find my location, so instead of sweeping the area with my cane I prodded with it. Would you believe, I prodded all around a big tree, couldn't feel anything, thought I was clear, went to walk forward and head butted a big tree.

People parking their cars on the pavement create quite a problem; they can't really complain if they find a few dents from the use of my cane caused when I am trying to find my way around the obstruction which they cause. I remember a visually impaired colleague of mine telling me about an incident which happened to him. He was walking along the pavement using his mobility cane in the normal way, when he encountered a car parked on the pavement blocking his way and whilst trying to find his way around this obstruction caught his hand on a projecting wing mirror which was fixed to the car. What he didn't realise was that he had cut his hand quite badly on this mirror. The first he knew about it was when he arrived at his destination, being greeted by his friends with shrieks of horror and exclaiming, "What on earth have you done? Your hand is covered in blood and what is making matters worse your light coloured raincoat is also covered in blood down one side where the blood has dripped from your hand." Not a nice experience.

I recall my first walk on my own using my long cane. It was around the block where we live, which I managed with not too much difficulty walking with the inshore line (the boundary line opposite the kerb line) on my left side. My left side being the side at that time where I had a little light perception and together with shadow vision at the extreme edge of my left eye makes this my strong side. The light was very good, quite bright which enhanced the shadows and thus made this first walk a little easier. Walking down Wainbody Avenue from the direction of the Kenpass Highway to find my house is not too difficult. My next door neighbour's fence is a good landmark as it consists of a tall (six foot) green privet hedge which has vertical overlap wooden board fencing terminating at about four foot in front of it. It's situated just before my drive and our fence is of identical construction also with a privet hedge, but yellow in colour, projecting from its top. Both however are about one foot lower than our neighbours'.

Just at the start of our drive is another positive land mark, a well established lime tree growing in the pavement, two foot from the down kerb. However, if I am walking down the avenue on the opposite side to my house, I locate the position I need to be at in order to cross the road and find my drive by observing the following:

> The house almost directly opposite ours has a wide open area which has crazy paving directly in front of it which is used for parking cars. The adjoining house has a low brick boundary wall which has a white coping stone on its top. Directly opposite the junction of the open crazy paved area and the low brick wall, very conveniently, is a street lamp, positioned at almost the kerb edge and facing directly my drive. Having located the low stone wall with its coping stone I turn through 90 degrees, feel for the street lamp and once confirmed, listen for traffic. If none can be heard I cross over, feeling with my cane for the up kerb, remembering that it will be a shallow one as it is the entry to my drive. I then continue to walk in the same direction, up my drive, until my cane locates my wrought iron drive gates which are fixed in line with the front of the house.

I found the perceptions of my sighted friends interesting who were all eager to assist me with their suggestions of how I could find my house, the most popular one being to count my footsteps from the highway or a known location in the avenue. I explained that this was not really practical because one needed all one's concentration in order to listen for both pedestrian and traffic noises and keeping an ever constant awareness for potential obstructions which the long cane may find. Another good reason for not counting steps is highlighted when one meets a friend who stops for a chat during your count; before acknowledging him you ask him to remember the number of steps that you have counted in case you forget when you continue on your way. The chances are, that after an interesting conversation you both forget or get it wrong which then can result in an embarrassing situation when one cannot find one's own home.

CHAPTER 8

MOBILITY - THE GUIDE DOG WAY

I MEET AND DEVELOP MY RELATIONSHIP WITH DORCAS

As I have said, in my life before eye problems and blindness my occupation was that of a sales and marketing executive. The UK sales office and the base for export sales was situated in Leamington Spa Warwickshire which also happened to be the Midland area training centre of The Guide Dogs for the Blind Association (GDBA). I well remember arranging and accompanying many a customer on visits to the GDBA training centre, particularly those who were generally interested in dogs, the visit making a welcome break in our business negotiations. This interest developed amongst both our customers and staff to the extent that we formed a small social group which had two objectives: to encourage social activities within the company and while having fun, we raised money for our local charity, which happened to be the GDBA.

I was very much involved with the organising committee for these events and raised £3000 over a period of time. A proud display was in the reception area of 3 silver Guide Dog statues which had been presented to the company. One is a German shepherd, which I am now proud to have in my possession. Visiting the GDBA I got to know various members of staff, including Carol, the receptionist/telephonist who was blind; she had her own Guide Dog with her, a black Labrador, who was always well behaved sitting in its basket near her feet. I met one or two blind people in training with their dogs and watched several films when we visited the training centre on visitors' afternoons which illustrated how blind people were able, with the aid of their Guide Dogs, to live normal lives.

I remember, in particular, a teacher who was able to continue his teaching career and what was more surprising, a farmer whose work had to be modified so as to remove the danger posed by machinery; to say I was impressed is an understatement. Little did I realise then that I would become blind and one day in the near future, I would myself be the proud owner of a Guide Dog. That experience and knowledge gained through my contact with the GDBA however was to become a major influence and support in my new life as a blind person. GDBA had shown me a positive way, through example, of how I could live a near normal life and I will always be grateful for that.

Right from the onset of my blindness I knew that a Guide Dog would provide for me the key to independence and the means of recovering that quality of life which I enjoyed as a sighted person. What I couldn't have appreciated, and other Guide Dog owners will understand what I mean, because you have to experience it, is that very special relationship which exists between the Guide Dog owner and their Guide Dog. It is virtually impossible to adequately describe those feelings of trust, confidence, love and companionship that build between the two of you. I had grown up with dogs ever since I was a little one in the pram. Dogs had been part of the family, so I had inherited this love of them, but never as I say could I have believed that one could experience such a close relationship with an animal as one has with one's own Guide Dog.

I am sure my first question to David Mumford when he made that first visit to my house to discuss my mobility training was, "I would like a Guide Dog, when can I have one and how do I apply?" So sure was I that a Guide Dog would help me that I found it very difficult to be patient while I was undergoing the long (mobility) cane training. I now realise of course how important it was to learn and become confident with a cane because while using the cane I was learning how to orientate myself and find my way about using my other senses. After all, one must remember that sometimes one doesn't want to take a Guide Dog everywhere, for instance the theatre. If the dog has an accident, cuts its pad on broken glass, something which sadly one finds all too often is left on the pavements these days, or is feeling unwell for a day or two, so if the dog is left at home the owner can still get around.

David Mumford made sure that I was fully confident with my long cane before he gave the go-ahead for me to apply to Guide Dogs. I really did hassle him though because by then I had started to attend the Guide Dog Training Centre in Leamington to give talks to the visitors about Guide Dogs and while doing so was finding out about the application procedures, hedging my bets one might say. I had a sneaky feeling that he wasn't all that keen on Guide Dogs, something I was to realise was quite common amongst social services personnel at that time; perhaps they saw them as some kind of job threat.

At long last my application was completed and submitted to Guide Dogs in Leamington, whereupon I waited, rather impatiently, for things to happen. Within a few weeks I received

chapter eight

a telephone call from Neil Ewart who at that time was in charge of training at GDBA at Leamington, advising me that he would like to come and visit me at home in order to discuss my application for a Guide Dog, so the date was fixed and the excitement began to build. I realise now that the purpose of this visit was really to find out what kind of person I was and what kind of living accommodation I had. It's very important that an accurate picture of the potential Guide Dog owner is compiled because the success of the match between the blind person and the Guide Dog depends upon it.

Take for instance, a man who works in an office, maybe in Birmingham, a large very busy industrial city, to which he would probably travel from home by bus to the local rail station and then on the train to Birmingham. This in complete contrast to maybe an elderly person who just goes down to the corner shop once a day, thus illustrating the two very different environments in which a dog could be working.

Neil's visit confirmed whether I lived in a flat or house. What kind of garden did it have, if any? Was there a park or fields near where the dog could free run? Did I live on my own or with family? Were there any small children in the family? Did we already have a dog? Was I used to handling dogs? Did the family like dogs? What was their reaction to the possibility of having a Guide Dog in the house? Did they realise that the responsibility for the dog would be mine, that I would be expected to look after the dog totally? Was the garden secure? Was there an area in the garden for the dog to use as its toilet? And so on.

The visit culminated with a walk along the avenue with Neil holding a Guide Dog harness in his right hand and me holding the harness handle in my left hand, with him telling me to imagine that he was a Guide Dog, which made me feel like a right Charlie. There was obviously a reason behind this exercise and that was to test the strength in my arms, a very important factor when assessing how well I was able to physically control a dog. The exercise involved us walking along the pavement to the first down kerb whereupon I was instructed to say 'sit'; all through the exercise Neil was holding the harness at around the height it would be if it were on a Guide Dog.

We crossed several road junctions in this manner during which Neil would weave about as though he was walking in and out of obstacles, a good way of testing how well I followed and maintained my grip on the harness handle. At times Neil would also stop and ask me to pull back on the handle. When I did this the first time I suppose I did it quite gently which wasn't what he wanted. He asked me to repeat the exercise and this time to try to yank his arm off and not to worry about hurting him. He seemed quite satisfied with the result and having completed both his interview and the physical test returned to Leamington advising me that I would be hearing from him in the near future. In the interim period I was asked to have a medical examination in order to confirm that I was fit enough to work with a Guide Dog and be also able to cope with the rigours encountered during the intensive training at the Guide Dog training centre.

I START MY GUIDE DOG TRAINING

Several months later that long anticipated day came, Friday November 18th 1987 to be exact, and at 11.30 on that day there I was standing in the reception area of the Guide Dogs for the Blind Association training centre at Emscote Manor Leamington Spa announcing my arrival. I was met by Mr Hamilton who took my case and introduced me to my room in which I was going to be sleeping for the next 4 weeks. I had previously been advised that during this period I would be learning how to be guided by a Guide Dog, how to cope with all the sorts of problems that I would be likely to encounter during every day life, how to look after my dog and most important of all give time for the dog to accept me and for the bonding between us to begin.

I would be living in the centre and would not be going home during this period and free time would be Sunday afternoons and evenings only. My family could visit me during these times but not during the first 2 weeks. This is an important time when the dog is getting to know its owner and distractions could unsettle it. Having found my room, a tour of the building then took place starting with the fire escape, then onto the lounge, dining room and lecture theatre. I remember being impressed by the importance being placed on the knowledge of safety within this new living environment, the staff ensuring that everyone knew exactly where the fire escapes where and the exit routes in the event of any emergency arising during our stay.

There were 10 of us on this class - we were called students - with 5 men and 5 women. We had arrived before lunch so we all assembled for lunch and introductions. It was an excellent meal and a good forerunner for what was to come. After lunch we all had another tour of the building, this time including the grooming room. It did cross my mind that a tactile plan of the living accommodation and other rooms would have been useful here. Again emphasis was placed on the safety aspects applied to the living environment and we were also shown the location of that special social place - the bar!

A talk followed which outlined the generalities of the course: the importance of getting to know the dog, and working together socially in harmony with each other, were points which were particularly stressed. We all met in the bar for a drink before dinner, the trainers treating us, thus providing more opportunities to relax and get to know each other. Dinner was followed by another talk, this time given by the house keeper, Mrs Chips as she was fondly known, about the domestic arrangements. It was quite an exciting first day, with everyone looking forward to getting their dog. At this stage no one knows what dog they have been allocated. We understand all will be revealed on Sunday after lunch; I can't wait. At 10.30 I retired to bed, tired but happy.

I slept reasonably well although the dogs outside in the kennel block roused me several times with their barking. What made me curious when this occurred was that they would all be barking together quite loudly and then suddenly all would be so quiet you could hear a pin drop.

Saturday morning, breakfast at 9.0 o'clock, we began work at 10, but I was up at 7.30 raring to go. Following a good cooked breakfast the morning was taken up with learning how to use the dog's guiding harness, the trainer acting as the dog, as on my test at home. We went around the two paddocks and learnt how to give the commands and the correct positioning of our bodies when handling the dog, attention being paid to foot positions, finding steps, both up and down, and corrections.

I walked, again with the trainer acting as the dog, through the training centre grounds, up and over the foot bridge and onto the Warwick New Road and back again. After lunch we were issued with various pieces of equipment; it was just like a lucky dip at Christmas time! We all sat in our chairs in the students' lounge whilst people came around giving out bits and pieces; one never quite knew what was coming next. We were given the harness in two pieces, the breast piece and the remainder and asked to assemble it, the final test being to put the harness over our knees, thus assuming the shape of the dog and then fixing the girth strap under our legs. Next was the lead and collar.

Having received this equipment we then stowed it in our lockers, identified in Braille, in the grooming room. I had an extra piece of equipment as I brought a pair of reflective waterproof over-trousers. Rene, a fellow student, had received a special harness of Swedish design, different from the standard design harness which the rest of us had received; the idea was that this harness would be better able to support a person who was unsteady on their feet.

My dog's trainer was David Thompson and today I gathered that both Reg, another fellow student, and I could have been allocated quite active dogs. David took us both down to the paddocks so that we became familiar with them, because our dogs will probably need a good run before going out to work to get rid of some of that exuberant spirit.

Tonight is the last night of so-called freedom as we receive our dogs tomorrow and then those burning questions will be answered. The excitement is really mounting now but the idea tonight is to have a quiet drink in the bar together because after this it may be difficult with our new friends beside us.

Sunday started off with strong winds and torrential rain, I dressed up in my waterproofs, wearing my waterproof trousers for the first time. We walked into Leamington, practising harness handling, with the trainers once again taking the place of the dogs. I felt very tense all morning in anticipation of receiving my dog after lunch. The morning wasn't too bad but I felt that I could have done better. Following our walk into Leamington, the session immediately before lunch was devoted to domestic training. This is done on the normal lead when the dog walks to heel and we learnt how to open doors and other obstacles without the dog catching its paws or tail.

Discussion over lunch was minimal, with everyone thinking about and anticipating the forthcoming afternoon's events. I found myself becoming quite nervous and tense, asking myself such questions as, am I doing the right thing? How will the dog get on with Pippa our little Shetland Collie dog at home? What breed will it be? Will it be a dog or a bitch? Will it be very active? Will I be able to cope? This is a major development in my new life.

Then at last, the moment I had waited and longed for was here. We had finished lunch and were sitting in anticipation back in the students' lounge, but first we were instructed how to behave when the dog was introduced, giving it runs and playing with it.

I MEET DORCAS FOR THE FIRST TIME

Then it happened. Our names were read out together with the name and details of the dog which we had been individually allocated. First were the 4 dogs trained by Phillipa; then the 3 trained by Kenny and then at last the 3 trained by David, my instructor. The first of David's dogs went to Sheila and then it was my name that was being called: "Eric Sayce you have a

chapter eight

German Shepherd bitch, her name is Dorcas". He didn't give any further details regarding colour and size, because evidently she was rather difficult to describe.

I don't know quite how I felt; I had been feeling very tense all day, this tension really building when the names were being read out. Secretly I had been longing for a retriever. I hadn't given a German Shepherd a thought, as I had the impression that only big, very active, tall men had these and yet here was I, of medium height, receiving one. What's more, I wasn't quite sure if I liked the idea of a German Shepherd as I had the impression that they were big aggressive guard-type dogs.

Evidently according to one of the student photographers afterwards, my face reflected my apprehension and they were a little concerned as to whether I considered it good or bad news. I really didn't know what to feel as I went up to my bedroom and sat in the chair at the bottom of my bed waiting for Dorcas to be brought up and introduced to me. Sitting there, I recalled hearing David saying to everyone, "Remember the dog makes friends with you, you don't make the first advances. Just sit there quietly in your chair and let the dog come to you." I thought to myself, have no fear I will.

As I sat there, waiting, I found myself thinking, I wonder what she will be like? Then as the reality of the situation dawned I found myself starting to make all sorts of plans. Will she be too big to go into the kitchen? How will she get on with little Pippa? What will Jean and Nicola think? They didn't want a German Shepherd, so will they like her?

Then at exactly 2.37pm on Sunday November 18th 1987 my bedroom door opened and in came David with Dorcas and she

134

is a beauty. Dorcas is a long haired German Shepherd, she is small for Shepherds, being about Labrador size. I suppose she comes up to just above my knee. She came in, took a sniff at me and then decided to explore my bedroom sniffing all around, on top of my bed and in her own bed which was situated just in front of where I was sitting. It was a plastic dog basket with a nice warm blanket in it. She evidently took a look out of the

Me and Dorcas

windows and then returned to me and the next thing I felt was a big paw on one knee and then another big paw on the other knee followed by a long wet tongue licking my face and beard, so I couldn't have looked that bad and that was Dorcas making friends, a moment I shall never forget.

I sat in my chair for a while listening to David describing Dorcas: she has attractive colouring, with a black muzzle, her forehead is a fair, light sandy brown colour with black flecks in it which extend around the eyes, a black back and very light fawn legs and a fawnish stomach. David then left us alone together saying he would give us half an hour to make friends after which I was to bring her down to the students' lounge and we would be told what was to follow next. The door closed and after a while Dorcas came up to me and sat down. I talked to her but didn't approach her as I remembered what we had been told: let her make friends with me. She started to nibble the chair cushion on which I was sitting so I thought now it's time to take out the rubber bone I had hidden up my jumper for her to play with. Immediately she saw it she grabbed it in her mouth, whereupon I got down on my knees on the floor with her and we played tug of war with it. After a few minutes playing I took the bone and put it away in the drawer of the clothes chest whereupon Dorcas went and sat in front of the drawer with her nose pressed firmly on it. I got it out again and we had more plays during which I started to gently pat and stroke her and gradually we began to make friends. What a surprise I had when I was feeling her: she wasn't big and hey! she has long hair. I hadn't realised German Shepherds had long hair. Within only a few minutes I began to have a lovely warm feeling about Dorcas. I sensed we were going to be alright. All apprehension and tension had evaporated, so now we could concentrate on getting to know each other.

The door opened in what seemed to be only a few minutes and Kenny came in with Dorcas's collar and lead which I put on her and off we all went down to the lounge.

In the lounge all the other students were assembling with their dogs. I found Dorcas to be quite a handful; she's obviously got lots of personality and go. She was very keen to discover what was going on, as I found it difficult to control her and unfortunately all the things that I had been taught in the morning went straight out of my head in the excitement. The chairs in the lounge were placed all around the edges of the room, leaving the centre clear of obstructions; in one corner there was a small bar with a sink and cupboards behind where coffee and tea was made. The chairs were placed with gaps between them in order that the Guide Dogs could sit in these, positioning themselves on the left hand side of their owner.

I sat down in my chair and Dorcas followed into the gap beside me, going in head first turning around and then lying down with her head resting on the floor between her front legs, staying there quite quietly with her ears pricked and head moving from side to side observing everything that was going on. The trainers made us a well deserved cup of tea after which we all went with our dogs back to our bedrooms and from here, out of the bedrooms again, using the doors leading onto the fire escape and taking them down it. This again emphasised the importance and need to be familiar with escape routes in the event of any emergency.

Dorcas wasn't too keen on walking down the fire escape; it was narrow, metal and obviously cold to her feet and the treads had holes in them through which Dorcas could see, which put her off. I don't think that she had been on that fire escape before but we managed alright. Following this exercise we practised obedience training, both in and around the house, opening and closing doors, making the dog sit clear whilst the door was opened, having remembered to knock on the door before opening it so as to warn anyone approaching from the other side. Then when the door was open calling the dog through; after some practice Dorcas seemed to be settling quite well and I was also beginning to get the hang of things.

chapter eight

Our first night together was uneventful. She was interested in what I was doing; first I put her into her bed and then turned out the light and got into mine. She seemed to settle as I heard her scraping her bed together and then I must have gone to sleep. I woke up in the middle of the night, wanting to go across to the toilet on the other side of the corridor. My first thought was I better not because I will disturb Dorcas but then I thought that's no good because I really need to go, so I got up. Dorcas, disturbed by my movements, also got up. I made a fuss of her and went across the corridor and on my return I made another fuss of her, put her back in her bed, got back into mine and off we both went to sleep again.

I was awakened by Irene, another fellow student, calling her dog, Quella, as she went along the corridor to the dog spending area. Dorcas had got up and was at the door sniffing, wondering what was going on. I looked at my watch and decided that at 6.30 we could have another quarter of an hour in bed. When we did get up I took Dorcas down to spend and this time she was very good and obedient, going through all the doors correctly.

MY FIRST DAY TRAINING WITH DORCAS

The morning began with grooming, which we did in the grooming room. Here grooming tables are provided, large flat surfaces raised about two feet off the ground, on which the dogs stand thus making it much easier to groom the dog as one doesn't have to bend one's back. Dorcas with her long coat is going to give me plenty of work to do, but she stood nice and quiet whilst I groomed her; evidently dogs like being groomed. There is a sequence of operations which we were taught and this helps to promote that bond between the dog and the blind person.

Following this we had another fire drill and this time Dorcas seemed happier on the fire escape. After this we all piled into the minibus and out into Leamington for our first experience of being guided by our dogs in harness. For this first walk David put his training harness on Dorcas which she was used to. I helped him do that and after a briefing of what we were going to be doing together, with reminders of how to use the harness, we set off. David also clipped a long lead to Dorcas's harness which he held during these first walks until I was accustomed to handling the harness. The first thing that I noticed is that, Dorcas walks at quite a brisk pace, but we seemed to be well suited and she behaved very well. I wonder what she thought of me?

I must admit it gives me a feeling of more independence; the only thing is you don't know what you are passing because the dog is taking you around all the obstacles which I used to feel with the white mobility cane, but it is a good feeling and I enjoyed it. Dorcas continues to become used to me and is now responding to my commands much better.

In the afternoon we had a talk about feeding the dogs from Nicole, the kennel manager, outlining the routine of feeding whilst the dogs are in the kennels and at home. In the training centre the dogs' food is prepared by the kennel staff, each dog having a personalised meal, which has been developed to suit it. It is placed in pigeon holes, situated in the grooming room, ready for us to collect, each pigeonhole being marked with the dog's name and the student's room number in Braille. Dorcas's dish was placed second from the right middle row. We were advised that ever since the dogs were with the puppy walkers they had been taught to sit and wait for a blast on the whistle before they were allowed to eat their food and that practice continues right throughout the dog's life.

Looking at my notes I recorded a piece about feeding Dorcas:

> I find the food in the pigeon hole, put it into Dorcas's feeding bowl then take both bowl and dog and find a quiet spot. I tell Dorcas to sit, then I put the food down in front of her covering the top of it with my hand and then move it slowly towards her at the same time telling her, "Leave". Next I blow the whistle, remove my right hand and tell her, "Okay, you can eat now". Dorcas is a delicate eater not a bit like the Labradors who are real Hoovers taking literally only a few minutes to polish off their meal and anyone else's if they get the chance.

Obedience training came next, which we did in the hangar which normally garages the transport. These exercises taught me how to encourage Dorcas to sit and stay while I walked away leaving her on her own; then if she stayed in that position until I returned I would pick up her lead, call her to heel, walk a few paces then ask her to sit whereupon if she had behaved I would give her lots of praise and encouragement. We were told that it was important to break the exercise in this way because if I had asked Dorcas to sit while I was in an office or at home then having left her for a while making a big fuss of her on my return, she wouldn't know when the exercise had finished. Dorcas did quite well in these exercises and I felt that we were beginning to develop an understanding for each other. The longer we are together the more in love, so to speak, I am becoming with her.

It was interesting to learn that Rene's dog in our class, a little Labrador, Quella, trained by Philipa, had been specially taught to give Rene confidence when negotiating stairs. Rene had a very good reason for hating stairs as she has fallen down them several times breaking various bones in the process, the latest being her knee. Quella has been trained that when ascending stairs she guides Rene to the bottom stair, stops and places both her front feet up on the first stair; in this position she waits for Rene to place her right foot on the same stair. This done Quella moves up to the next one, Rene brings her left foot up and onto this stair, thus repeating the exercise until the top one is safely reached; needless to say Rene is thrilled with her dog.

The first few nights we had been advised to put the collars on our dogs and attach the lead when we put them to bed in our bedrooms so that they were anchored and wouldn't disturb us too much, but after a while I left Dorcas free in the room when we both went to bed. I would settle her in her bed first and she was perfectly okay. I remember waking up a couple of mornings at around 3.0 am and putting my hand out of the bed and feeling a big muzzle at my side. I didn't take any notice and after a while she would go back to her basket and settle down again, but when I awoke at around 6 and swung my feet out of bed I would find her lying full length by the side of my bed like a nice warm rug. At 6.30 I would take her down for a run.

FURTHER TRAINING

Dorcas when walking on the lead at heel, was always trying to pull and being a strong dog she can exert quite a pull which I had taught to counter by letting the lead go slack and then jerking it back quite sharply so that the choke chain pinches her neck and produces a sudden sharp reminder that she should not pull, at the same time giving the command *heel*. At first I was quite concerned that this could hurt Dorcas but David explained that the dogs have a lot of thick loose flesh around their necks. He said if you observe dogs at play together they always go to grab each other by that loose skin around the neck and now by doing this correction Dorcas is beginning to accept that I am in control.

The first time that we did obstacle training Dorcas was very good but she had a habit of cutting things a bit fine, only leaving clearance of around four inches on my shoulder; her whole attitude was a bit flippant. On one of the walks through the obstacles which were barriers across the pavement, coned off areas, Miss Wild suddenly appeared which gave me quite a surprise because I walked straight in to her. Dorcas was checked for that and following this incident she concentrated and was very good, looking at the obstacles and taking me well clear of them when we did this route through the obstacles seven or eight times.

I remember that on approaching the obstacles for the first time, I had put Dorcas in the *sit* and then the *down* positions and commanded her to *stay* whilst David walked me through the obstacles in order that I had an idea of what was involved. We did this four or five times and Dorcas stayed in position during all of this even staying when I returned to her, which I thought was very good. She was very pleased to see me on my return, which also gave me a very nice feeling and of course she received lots of praise and fuss.

During one of our lessons about equipment, we were given the opportunity to purchase extras at discount prices from the local GDBA supplier. I took advantage of this offer, buying a stainless steel feeding bowl and a sterilised bone; the bone seemed to be very good and had a pleasant smoked smell. I was even tempted to try it myself, it felt clean and dry with a textured surface and there were knuckles at each end rather like the rubber play bone which I had brought with me. It was perfectly suitable for inside the house as the sterilising process had removed the grease. Dorcas enjoyed it as a treat and it was good for her as the action of gnawing it helped clean her teeth.

Through my various contacts with the GDBA I had been hearing snippets of information which were beginning to lead me to believe that Dorcas has a brother called Daniel. One morning when Nicole was treating Dorcas's elbows, (incidentally all the dogs receive a thorough examination each morning) I asked her if it was true; she smiled and was rather evasive at first, eventually laughing and asking, "How do you know that? How did you find out?" I replied that no one from the centre had told me, but that I had deduced it by using the limited knowledge of GDBA systems that I had acquired.

Yes, Dorcas had a brother called Daniel. He was almost a twin and qualified on the class before ours; he was about two years old which dated Dorcas for me and he lived in Milton Keynes, where his owner is a professor at the Open University. This meant that he does a lot of travelling around the country, so Dorcas comes with good connections. All the puppies born in the same litter are named with names beginning with the same letter, so Daniel fitted in with Dorcas; another interesting point, which helped confirm my suspicions, was that both Daniel and Dorcas are biblical names. Dorcas was of particular relevance for me as the translation is *full of good works*, which she has proved herself to be for me in so many different ways.

Our social life was well provided for during our stay in the training centre. In addition to the story swapping in the bar in the late evenings, where we mixed with staff and students, outside activities were also arranged. One of these activities was ten pin bowling at a rink in Coventry, the trainers when they played, were blind folded of course. Needless to say, we students won. Another evening we all, including the trainers, walked down to a pub in Warwick, leaving the dogs back in the centre. Then, as a sign of our, the students' appreciation of the work and time given to us by our trainers, we organised a party in the training centre for them, Kenny Hamilton bringing along a group of folk singers from Kenilworth to entertain us.

Walking with Harry in harness

TRAINING IN THE TOWN

Up until now our training outside the centre had been around the quieter suburban streets of Leamington but now we were going to work the dogs in the actual town. The dogs were harnessed up and for this first walk in town the trainers accompanied us, clipping their long check leads to the dogs as well. This was the first time that we had come into contact with the public and real street furniture in a town environment.

David took the opportunity during this walk to draw my attention to the fact that a vehicle, which has its engine running was emitting exhaust fumes which are obnoxious to the dog which has its nose usually at the same height as that of the vehicle's exhaust pipe and the dog's sense of smell is around fifty times more sensitive than our own human noses. He pointed out that we should try to avoid crossing directly behind such a vehicle.

At one point David suggested I take his elbow, at the same time releasing the harness handle so that it now lay on Dorcas's back. This action indicated to Dorcas that she was no longer responsible for guiding me and that David had taken over, so she reverted to walking to heel. At the first *down* kerb I halted and waited for David to check that it was safe for us to cross a busy road and then return back to the minibus.

This experience of being guided by Dorcas was great, very positive; the way she weaved in and out of the pedestrians and other obstacles really gave me confidence. David told me that Dorcas had had her ears right back indicating that she was really concentrating on her work, as opposed to their normal upright position.

After about a week together during which time the confidence was building each with the other, Dorcas began to feel that she could begin to take advantage of me in some situations, doing her own thing and not concentrating on my commands. We had been involved in obstacle avoidance work and Dorcas really had not been concentrating, being much more interested in looking around to see what the other dogs were doing and trying to take me further down the road in the direction of the park where she evidently thought that she would get a free run. David had been observing this and instructing me on how to counter this but when Dorcas went too far, he suddenly came and yanked back on the lead, pinching her neck causing her to yelp. "Don't worry about it, it doesn't hurt her," he said. "She's really testing you to see how far she can go; all the dogs go through this phase so it has to be nipped in the bud." Dorcas got the message immediately as she stopped misbehaving and worked perfectly.

Harry with me waiting to cross a road

Then came the moment when we had progressed sufficiently to be allowed to go out on our own, without the trainers tailing us. I hasten to add however that we were still being supervised and under observation as the trainers substituted foot power for motor power. They would set us a route to follow and then drive around this route in their cars observing us. During the later stages of the route we came across a dog barking quite furiously behind a fence on the nearside. Dorcas slowed right down as we approached it but with my encouragement *"up-up-up* find the way" she did. We also experienced some more youngsters, this time whistling at us, but again I was able to maintain Dorcas's concentration on where she was guiding me, eventually arriving back at the minibus.

I made the following recording:

> Well into our training now and all the Labradors are sitting at the doors and negotiating them without the need to reinforce the commands. Dorcas does so rather reluctantly; in other words when I look in her direction she does but if she thinks she can get away without doing so she will. German Shepherds are obviously more difficult to win over, but once you have won them over they are evidently a very loyal dog, a one person dog. There are quite a number of cats living in the training centre along with the dogs. These cats play an important role in the training of the dogs, who get used to them walking around and teasing them, particularly it seems when we are all assembling on the terrace before moving off at the start of our exercises. The cats seem to know that this is our assembly point and take great delight in congregating there, normally on the steps of the fire escape just above and out of reach of the dogs, but the dogs ignore them. Dorcas went so far as to sniff one of these cats the other day which evidently was a fairly new one. The cat stood its ground and Dorcas didn't seem interested in chasing it, which is important when one considers the disastrous effect that could have on me if she tried to chase a cat whilst she was guiding me. Dorcas is getting to know me better. She now rolls over onto her back and lets me tickle her tummy.

THE FAMILY MEET DORCAS

The family got to meet Dorcas on the second weekend of the course. I had already told them on the telephone about Dorcas and of course they were very excited to hear what dog I had been given, but it was with more than a little concern that I had broken the news because I knew that they didn't like German Shepherds. In their opinion they were big, aggressive guard type dogs and the idea of me actually having one we had considered to be very remote. Jean's concern and dismay was very evident in the tone of her voice on the other end of the telephone even though I had described Dorcas as being a small German Shepherd.

As I have said, I had rather fancied a retriever, but how wrong was my impression of German Shepherds and how grateful I have subsequently been to the person who matched me with Dorcas.

The second Sunday afternoon came, the time for the families to meet the dogs. Nicola was working an early shift that day so she and Jean came in the evening arriving at around 6.45. Instead of it being that anticipated exciting evening that I had hoped, it turned out to be very much of an anti-climax and charged with tension. I followed the procedures as we had been directed by our trainers, taking Dorcas down into the run and then showing Jean and Nicola into my bedroom and explaining to them what was to happen. I then went down and collected Dorcas and brought her up to my room. When I opened the door Dorcas came in, immediately showing a very keen interest in who was in the room. She looked around for a minute or so but didn't seem to be very sure, a situation which she confirmed by giving a little low growl. She walked around, didn't sniff, then went and sat in the corner under the window by the sink from which position she examined us closely with her eyes. I then went and stood in front of Jean and Nicola who were sitting on the bed. Dorcas then came and squeezed between the back of my legs and the chest against which I was leaning, where she stayed for about a quarter of an hour, looking very timid and not a bit happy about the visitors being in the room.

I then took her down into the grooming room where there was a lot more space and Nicola started to make friends with her. Dorcas was still a little hesitant at first but then started to wag her tail and sniff, but she wouldn't have anything to do with Jean at any price. We all then went into the students' lounge, where she still didn't take any notice of Jean and Nicola; from there we went into the quiet room where we sat for the rest of the evening. Dorcas really wasn't very interested; she lay with her front paw on Nicky's shoe and her head on my foot, but with Jean, no contact at all. My problem was that Jean thought that Dorcas had taken a dislike to her, thus confirming her negative impressions of German Shepherds, she also thought she's big and would eat Pippa when she came home.

Jean was very concerned about the situation, over-anxious really, which caused a lot of tension and friction between us, which I am sure Dorcas was picking up, which wasn't helping the situation. In a way I wish that they hadn't come in the evening; I would rather we had met as we originally planned in the afternoon, because then Dorcas could have free run in the paddock and probably made friends much quicker that way.

chapter eight

German Shepherds are also very sensitive and Dorcas could probably smell Jean's fear as evidently when we are frightened, we produce adrenaline which the dogs with their sensitive noses can scent, a throw back from their hunting days.

I remember recording the following:

> Now I found myself worrying about Dorcas's relationship with Pippa or Pippa's relationship with Dorcas, Dorcas fitting in at home and all the problems that could mean. In a way it emphasises what I was worrying about before I came, how would Jean accept a larger dog? We parted on an angry note, and I thought I might see them again sometime towards the end of the week.

> I felt very unhappy because everything that I seem to do I get a problem with. Jean hasn't really accepted my blindness yet, she won't bend, she will not accept that life has to change and I do try hard not to be selfish because I am the cause. I seriously wonder whether I should continue with Dorcas, but give the opportunity to someone else who can handle the situation better than I. If I do that however I have lost a big opportunity for independence for the rest of my life. What price independence, I ask myself?

PROGRESS WITH MY FAMILY AND WITH THE TRAINING

In the evening Jean and Nicky came and this time our meeting place with Dorcas was the grooming room with David present. When I brought Dorcas down to meet them David gave Jean some doggy treats, yeast tablets, with which to tempt Dorcas but she still didn't seem very keen to make friends, so we all moved into the bar and here she started to make a few little gestures towards Jean so we moved into the quiet room; here Dorcas began to feel happier with Jean. She started to sniff her a few times and wag her tail, but she obviously can still smell Jean's tension although things are improving and this time when we parted we were all feeling much happier.

To round off this particular evening Kenny Hamilton had arranged that some friends of his from Kenilworth, a folk group of which he is a member, entertain us, staff and students alike, with plenty of opportunities for us all to join in. It was a great relaxing evening with the dogs also joining in the singing and it was during their singing that I realised that in addition to her other talents Dorcas has a powerful singing voice but one that was in need of a little fine tuning. I think she enjoys music, but whether we enjoyed her singing is a different matter.

Country walks and free running

Next was an exercise with a difference, Country Walks, using the Guide Dogs out in the country lanes where there are no pavements. The weather was rather miserable, dull and rainy with large puddles and mud everywhere. The lane was long and narrow with only turnings into fields or farm gateways. For the first time in training we brought our long mobility canes, the idea being to use these to *trail* behind us as we were walking, holding it in the right hand together with the dog's lead, the lead being used to reinforce commands and the harness handle to hold purely for guidance.

When one hears a vehicle approaching, one drops the harness handle and gets the dog off the road and onto the grass verge as quickly as possible, having first checked the verge is safe to stand on by prodding around it with the long cane. Dorcas and I led the group along this lane and when the first vehicle approached I carried out this procedure. Of course as soon as Dorcas was on the grass verge she started sniffing the grass and found an object which she picked up in her mouth and started to chew. I told her to drop it, which she did, what was it? A toothbrush of all things!

Next morning, Thursday, into Leamington again, but this time on the minibus and walk back, pausing to free run the dogs in the park on our own. Dorcas is beginning to behave quite well and I can now feel when she's not paying attention and my resulting corrective commands appear to be doing the trick; David seems to be pleased with our progress. "Dorcas is really well tuned into you now", he said. Evidently I am making the right kind of corrections, matching voice with right kind of hand movements.

In the afternoon, another free running session, this time at Newbold Common, a large expanse of open common land situated on the eastern outskirts of Leamington On the approach to the common there are a number of small concrete sleeping policemen which make traffic reduce its speed when entering the common. When we were approaching the common in the bus the dogs were all lying quietly on the floor but as soon as we hit that first sleeping policeman all hell let loose. The dogs, who obviously had been there before, immediately sprang to their feet, recognising where they were and in full anticipation of what was to come.

Dorcas had started to whine and talk ever such a lot and really I had to keep her quiet, lifting her up by the scruff of her beard and telling her firmly, "Quiet", while at the same time staring her straight in the eye; eye ball to eye ball, is the correct way of doing it. However brutal this method may seem to be, in fact it is not. David explained that it was quite in order to use this method, but what he would never tolerate under any circumstances would be someone hitting a dog in the face, because that *is* cruel and if he saw anyone doing such a thing, they would be off the class immediately.

On this occasion we were joined by a training van with around half a dozen dogs in their early stages of training. When this van drew up alongside us you could hear the dogs going mad inside barking and pawing at the sides of the van in anticipation of getting out for a run. At this time we were out of the bus with our dogs in the *sit* position on the edge of the car park. The dogs in training were released first and boy, oh boy, to try and hold our dogs back from joining in was almost a super human effort. The dogs were all hyped up, trembling all over like jelly with the sheer excitement and anticipation of free running; their natural instincts had taken over and any thought of control from us had gone out of the window.

We were in fact reminded and shown how to control our dogs in the *sit* and *down* positions whilst they were in this state of high anticipation, thus preventing them running off even when taunted by the other dogs and particularly when the other dogs in our group were let off individually. It was a very good lesson and test of obedience. While the dogs in training were chasing each other around the common we were walking our dogs to heel around the car park. We also made them sit and stay, doing this with their play collars on. Dorcas is good on the recall, coming back at first call each time and I obviously made a great fuss of her when she did.

After they had been running for a while we called them and put them in the *down* position, told them to stay and then walked all around them at a distance of about 10 paces; both Dorcas and Quinton stayed put which was a good test. We also put them into the *sit* position, told them to *stay* and walked away, then from quite some distance shouted the command *down*. When I did this, it was funny because both dogs went down, Quinton as well as Dorcas, which only goes to show that it's not so much the voice, as the emphasis in the way the command is projected. The dogs were then allowed to roam as a pack whilst David took Reg on one arm and me on the other for a walk around the common; the other trainers did likewise with their students.

During a free run we were introduced to a favourite pastime of Labradors. One of the group had discovered a small pond of stagnant water and immediately plunged in and wallowed in it, eventually coming out covered in brown and very, very smelly slime, which it then proceeded to distribute all over its owner by shaking itself vigorously. Another favourite of some dogs is to find the smelliest of deposits in a field and roll in them, so we had been warned; however it is one way of getting a seat and compartment to yourself on a crowded train as happened to a Guide Dog owner friend of mine.

Another session dealt with instructing us how to fill in the report forms which are required to be completed after we have qualified and the dogs are working with us at home. The trainers together with their supervisors keep a close eye on the dog's behaviour when it first leaves the training centre. The reports, which we have to complete and return to the centre, one each week for the first 4 weeks and then one at the beginning of each month for 12 months, cover the dog's quality of work and behaviour, any sign of difficulties, however slight and the trainers visit you in order to check both you and the dog with a view to correcting any problem which may be developing; this is a very reassuring and an effective back-up and after-care service.

In addition to this facility, after-care includes visits to the Guide Dog owner's home at regular intervals; these are determined by the competence of both dog and Guide Dog owner working as a unit. There is emphasis placed on safety when exposed to traffic, so the traffic tests experienced in training using the Guide Dog cars are again carried out, serving to test and sharpen both Guide Dog and Guide Dog owners' reaction in these situations. The time intervals are shorter during the early stages of the dog settling in and getting to know its work patterns and area. The same applies as a dog reaches retirement time in order to check when this should occur, thus ensuring the dog can live to enjoy a stress free, well earned retirement. It also enables the selection of a replacement dog to commence without time pressure.

One afternoon I saw Pam and Sue, both volunteers on the visitors' committee. They were looking after a group of Brownies from Derby and asked me if I could call in and see them after I had finished the first part of the afternoon's training. I checked with David and he said yes, providing that I didn't let the Brownies crowd Dorcas. So having finished training in time I took Dorcas into the lecture theatre to meet them. I let the Brownies come up to Dorcas, one at a time and have a stroke of her. I'm not sure who was the most excited, Dorcas or the Brownies. Dorcas was certainly very interested in them, hopefully a sign of things to come. Both Pam and Sue seemed delighted that I had got Dorcas; they obviously liked her and said that we looked a good match.

One brightish morning, no frost but quite cold, was a nice morning for walking, but at the end of the walk I was unsure of where the steps into the centre grounds were located. At a point where I thought they must be near I started to say to Dorcas, "Find the steps, find the steps, good girl, find the steps", when suddenly she crossed over in front of me and stopped and there, when I put my foot to feel, lo and behold were the steps. I praised her well making a big fuss of her, she wagged her tail and we both enjoyed the moment.

In the afternoon Jean and Nicola came to visit. Dorcas seems to be friendly with Jean now, so we took Dorcas down to the paddock for her to have a run and she was running back and forth to Jean who was feeding her with Pet Tabs so all is shaping up well.

Dorcas took me by surprise one day, when towards the bottom of Kenilworth High street she suddenly turned across in front of me to the right and stopped; she wagged her tail and seemed quite pleased with herself. I gently put both my foot and hand out feeling for what I thought must be an obstruction. As my hand touched what appeared to be a door, it opened and a man stepped out towards me. As he passed me the man called out "You've got him trained well, mate," and laughed. I was completely confused. "Where am I?" I called. "Why you're outside the Green Man," he replied. On reflection afterwards I thought to myself, a Guide Dog that can find pubs, it's a bonus which I hadn't anticipated. I kept asking myself how did she know? I didn't have to wait long for the answer; when I told David at the end of the walk, he said "Oh no, I should have warned you. I often pop into the Green Man for a drink, it's my local and on some of the visits Dorcas has been with me. She must have thought that you were in need of one."

ANIMAL PSYCHOLOGY

Our training programme was structured so as to provide us with welcome breaks from the physical exercise. This was interspersed with lecture sessions dealing with subjects such as animal psychology, health, feeding and after care routines and services, plus the Guide Dogs Association's support and active involvement in other areas relating to blind welfare.

I found the animal psychology of particular interest. It is obviously essential for the dog trainers to have a sound understanding of how the dog thinks and behaves but it also vital for us Guide Dog owners to appreciate the subject in order that we are able to control our dogs and maintain their performance levels. It was explained that all dogs are pack animals within which they have a pack leader. In a Guide Dog owner's family the pack leader is the Guide Dog owner. It is very important that only the Guide Dog owner controls the dog and not the family and gives commands to the dog and is responsible for the care, actually doing the grooming, giving the medicinal tablets when necessary and most important of all, the feeding of the dog; this latter point is important as it helps to maintain the bond between Guide Dog owner and the dog.

After this it was interesting to note how Dorcas responded to the individual members of my family when I got home, treating the family as a pack, putting us in levels of seniority and responding accordingly. Whenever I was around then I was the pack leader; if we were all sitting in the lounge and Dorcas was misbehaving then either Jean or Nicola would tell me and I would correct Dorcas who then responded correctly, but if either of them corrected her she would ignore them. Now if I was not in the lounge when Dorcas was misbehaving, Jean would correct her but Dorcas would ignore her; however if Nicola corrected her then she would respond correctly. With Jean in the lounge on her own with Dorcas misbehaving, then when Jean corrected her she would respond correctly. It is not difficult to deduce from this information that Dorcas had very quickly worked out the pecking order in my house: me as pack leader, followed by Nicola and then Jean (Jean wasn't impressed!)

DORCAS AND I BECOME A TEAM

Another sense of achievement which I will never forget occurred when one afternoon two weeks into the training I suddenly realised that Dorcas was now accepting me, the bond between us was beginning to develop. It was a special experience, a warm and loving feeling, with a touch of pride and belonging. In order to understand it however, you really do have to experience it. Why? When David came into the lounge with the other trainers to brief us on the next stage of our training I suddenly realised that Dorcas had remained lying by my side; she had made no effort at all to get up or even creep along the floor on her tummy to David who up to now had obviously been her idol. In these early days it would be true to say that Dorcas tolerated me, but in her people pack at that time David was definitely the pack leader and she loved him. She was always seeking his attention and trying to get near him for a bit of fuss.

All the dogs on the class behaved in similar ways towards their trainers; looking back it must have been quite funny watching their antics as they tried to win back the love and attention of their trainers, friends who seemed to have deserted them. When we first had our dogs, whenever the trainers came into the lounge the dogs would immediately jump up and run to them wagging their tails and making a good deal of fuss, obviously pleased to see them.

I could just imagine the thoughts running through Dorcas's head: "What are you doing? Why have you left me with this man? He's blind, he can't see where he's going or what he's doing and he's telling me what to do. You and I have had some good times playing and working together, so what's going on?" The trainers of course, were very much aware of these situations and conscious that the bond between the dog and themselves now needed to be transferred to the Guide Dog owner. You can probably imagine the fuss and upheaval going on at these times with the trainers shouting to us students, "Control your dogs, will you please control your dogs, call them back to you, they are your responsibility now, you must not let them come to us." Well you can imagine, I called Dorcas and another dog came to me, whilst Dorcas took the opportunity to check someone else out, and also stopped to have a chat with another dog.

Today however, just two weeks into our training together, she didn't do any of those thing and she stayed by my side, well behaved. I guessed that she was looking up at me and probably thinking to herself, "What's the point, I am only going to be told off if I go to David. I suppose Eric isn't too bad even if he does snore in his sleep and after all he is feeding me. I reckon I could get to like him." This was another of those experiences that I will never forget as this was an indication that Dorcas was beginning to accept me as her pack leader - we were beginning to bond. It was a moment which made me feel extremely emotional, warm and loving towards Dorcas, all the hard work was beginning to pay off.

Control of our dogs in social situations was now being gradually introduced into our training. We were now taking our dogs into the dining room at meal times on a regular basis, making them lie under the table whilst we had our meals. Dorcas behaved very well in these situations; she was quiet, ignoring most of what was going on around her, except of course if David sat at the table, then she tried to attract him and I was told to control her and make her concentrate on only me. When we had one or two other dogs sharing the space under the table including on the odd occasion a foreign dog (a member of staff's own pet dog or another trainer's dog in training) arguments used to break out between the dogs as to who was sitting in whose space and again a pack leader element came into play. If a scrap of food was dropped onto the floor during the meal, there was immediately a huge commotion and scramble by the dogs under the table as they disputed whose it was, the Labradors winning every time, eating first and arguing after. Dorcas, I am grateful and pleased to say, seemed only interested in exploring and sniffing and did not take food. She held her own ground against the other dogs, however being at times very vocal and bossy; in fact I think that she could be a bit of a bully. When these commotions erupted and I am sure they were very often trainer-inspired as part of our training, we were scolded by the trainers and told to control our dogs.

DORCAS MEETS PIPPA

By now Dorcas and Jean were getting to know each other a little better, Dorcas becoming much more settled and friendly towards Jean. One big problem still remains however, how will

Dorcas and Pippa get on together? How will we introduce them to each other?

We didn't have to wait long for the answer, as David advised us that the time was now right to be thinking of introducing the dogs to each other. The following weekend was agreed and the place was the paddock run at the training centre - neutral ground. It was very important that neither dog should feel threatened when the introduction took place, hence the paddock, which also provided plenty of enclosed space for the dogs to run about; they would be on their own with no other dogs about.

Jean was obviously very nervous at the thought of this meeting, fearing for Pippa's safety and I must admit I was a little apprehensive too. Jean arrived with Pippa during Saturday afternoon equipped with a strong collar and lead for Pippa. I met them in reception and it was good to see Pippa again and she was obviously pleased to see me; her whole body was wriggling and her tail wagging like crazy as I made a big fuss of her.

During this time Dorcas was up in my bedroom. David was on hand for this first introduction and he introduced himself to Pippa and then with Jean and Pippa went down to the paddock. I went up to my room and collected Dorcas; she was obviously very interested in me as she could smell Pippa's scent. I joined Jean and Pippa with David down in the paddock, both dogs being on leads. Then under David's watchful eye and instruction we allowed them to sniff each other and make friends, gradually letting the leads out as they became more familiar with each other.

chapter eight

Pippa appeared to be showing the most interest, not being at all afraid of Dorcas who is three times her size. After a while David suggested that we let both dogs off their leads. At this point Jean expressed concern, but David reassured her and suggested that I let Dorcas off first. This I did whereupon Dorcas ran off down to the bottom of the paddock. Then, what a surprise little Pippa turned out to be! A forward little madam, not a bit afraid but wanting to join in this game of running about. She started to jump up and down and pulling very hard on her lead to the point where Jean bent down and held her collar. This wasn't to put little Pippa off however, with the result that her strength of purpose was such that she broke her collar, something that she had never done before and was off to join Dorcas. Both dogs were now free and despite Jean's frantic screams to Pippa to come back both dogs were having fun chasing each other about the paddock. I had never known little Pippa run about so much, obviously enjoying herself.

After a while I called Dorcas and rather reluctantly she came to me with Pippa following. Jean called Pippa but in the end had to physically collect her whereupon both dogs were put back on leads, the end of a very successful exercise and afternoon, sighs of relief all round I can tell you. It looks as if things are going to work out alright. The dogs seem to get on well together here but what about when I take Dorcas home at the end of training? I asked David, "How will Pippa react then? After all, it's her own territory."

"There is a procedure which we use in these situations, one which I suggest you follow". He then explained: "At about the time that you are due home with Dorcas Jean should take Pippa out into the back garden and let her play there. When you arrive home with Dorcas take her into the house on her lead through the front door, keeping Dorcas on the lead. Let her explore the rooms in which she will be allowed, then settle her, still on the lead, in the lounge. Jean should then go and collect Pippa, put her on the lead and let her come back into the house under her own steam. Because Dorcas will already be in the house she will be signalling dominance, "It's my house now," which Pippa will accept and having already met each other they should settle down together. After a while, judging on how the dogs are behaving, let Pippa off the lead first and then some time afterwards Dorcas and encourage them to go out and play in the garden." Sounds OK but we shall see how it works in practice, fingers crossed.

We needn't have worried as it worked out just as David said it would.

For more about my Guide Dogs see Chapter 9 on *My Four Best Friends*.

A POSITIVE JOURNEY

PREFACE TO PART 2
Julia Ionides and Peter Howell,
The Dog Rose Trust

Eric has worked with us at the Dog Rose Trust for over 20 years and has been a valued consultant on numerous jobs: *Cathedrals Through Touch and Hearing*, the interactive model of the Palace of Westminster, audio walks around villages and towns and many more.

In Part 2 of this book Eric describes, through a variety of projects, how he learnt to live and enjoy life again. He begins to explore and test the limiting factors created by his situation and through this his other senses are rediscovered and exploited.

Eric's aim has been to show that people who are blind and visually impaired can lead full lives and that blindness is no obstacle to taking part in a wide range of activities.

Although his participation in some of these activities took place some years ago, their importance and relevance still has the same aim – inclusion for all.

Over the years events and facilities for people who are blind have increased but not as much as they should. The impetus for such provision has to come from the blind community themselves, but the present economic problems this makes harder.

Eric has been a leader for many of the projects described here and has been an inspiration for people who have lost their sight in middle life.

Eric's Guide Dogs have always been an important part of our team. Very early in our working partnership with Eric we were in Hereford Cathedral checking the script for the route around it. Dorcas, Eric's first Guide Dog, tried to squeeze him between a large column and the font, causing him to catch his foot on the font's base. Eric told Dorcas to think again; she backed him away, looked around and chose a safer route for him.

The font at Hereford Cathedral

It was our first experience of the incredible intelligence of Guide Dogs and we were very impressed and remain impressed every time we work with one. They are all included in the Chapter on *My Four Best Friends*.

Note: The name Dog Rose Press was chosen by Peter for publishing books and registered in 1981. Dog Rose continued with other activities such as recording and producing CDs. It therefore predates our involvement with people who are blind and Guide Dogs by some thirty years, but does cause some confusion!

CHAPTER 9

MY FOUR BEST FRIENDS

Four of my best friends have been four legged ones, German Shepherd Guide Dogs in fact. Since becoming blind in 1985 they have helped me to turn my life around, giving me confidence, independence and a purpose to live again. It is impossible to describe that special bond which develops between the Guide Dog and its blind owner. One cannot express in words that extraordinary relationship with each one being dependent on the other. This chapter gives just a glimpse of the personalities and characteristics of the dogs I have had the privilege to own and work with.

I have already written about how I trained with my first Guide Dog, Dorcas, who was very exceptional in so many ways, as the first dog always is. That's the one which gives you the independence and confidence to get out and about from the safety of home. Dorcas lived up to her name; Dorcas is a Greek biblical name which means full of good works and for me Dorcas obviously was.

At this time I was chairing the fund raising committee for equipment for the Resource Centre for the Blind in Earlsdon Avenue South in Coventry. We managed to raise £180,000 in just over eighteen months and the money was used to equip the centre. My philosophy has always been that people like a winner, so consequently I made sure that we always got a lot of coverage in the media, especially at cheque presentations which of course resulted in Dorcas getting her photograph taken. She liked this, particularly the interest which she generated. She liked being the centre of attention and quickly developed a nose for photographers, which she could spot a mile away, whereupon she immediately would go into a pose. Dorcas had one habit however which could be rather frustrating and annoying at times, but this habit is quite common in German Shepherds: she never stopped talking or, as I rather preferred to call it, *whingeing*.

We eventually came to an arrangement however that I would allow her to *whinge* providing she would not *whinge* when I was talking. I was able to turn this around when I gave talks to the public by telling them before I commenced my talk not to be surprised if Dorcas interrupted me at some point; the reason being that she had heard my talk many times and could spot a mistake, whereupon she would interrupt me. When this happened I would look at her and ask, "Well what should I have said?" At which point she would reply, so this worked out as a happy compromise.

My favourite use of Dorcas in this way was when I gave a presentation immediately following a good lunch. People would settle in their chairs feeling quite comfortable and relaxed and someone inevitably would doze off. On these occasions I would warn my audience that if they dared to sleep during my presentation then Dorcas would be watching and would tell me. Of course someone would succumb. This would result in the person sitting next to them, who was paying attention to my talk, hearing the snores. They would give the offending person a dig in the ribs causing that person to wake up with a splutter and at the same time they were told that Dorcas had spotted them. Of course the people in the immediate vicinity had anticipated what would happen, which caused lots of amusement.

Dorcas checking the plan of York Minster with me

Dorcas in addition to liking to be the centre of attraction was also very nosy. I remember one occasion when I was working with my friends Peter and Julia of the Dog Rose Trust, checking a three dimensional tactile plan of York MInster which had been produced by the Trust. The plan was mounted on a wooden base which was supported on a desk. I was standing looking down on the plan with my hands outstretched on either side of its base. Dorcas was situated on the opposite side of the plan to me and being nosey jumped up onto her hind legs to see what I was doing. She steadied herself by placing her front feet on the plan, directly opposite my hands. Peter saw an opportunity and took a photograph of Dorcas and me both looking down on the plan. This photograph was later used in all the Trust's publicity material, including the Internet, as the project was named The Dorcas Project in recognition of her involvement with me.

Sadly Dorcas went to sleep before she had a chance to enjoy a well earned retirement; she was ten and a half years old and we had been together for eight and a half fantastic years. She suddenly developed a tumour in her chest and within a few days she went to rest with her head in my lap nursing her favourite toy, a *kong*, six months before she could have retired. Truly a very special friend.

With Harry at Mitchell's Fold Stone Circle in Shropshire

Harry was my second Guide Dog, a male German Shepherd weighing 43 kilos. He was of a challenging disposition but unlike Dorcas, who was long haired, Harry was short haired. Harry was tall with long legs and Shepherd colours of black and tan and he possessed a typical *macho* personality. His idea of fun, when he was free running was, in addition to rounding up any unsuspecting stray Guide Dogs, to play a game similar to what I knew as *Chicken*. This was played by Harry, being some distance from you, suddenly turning and running straight at you at full speed, then at the very last minute just as you braced yourself for the crash he would swerve away missing you by a hair's breadth.

Harry and I finding out about walks at the Bury Ditches in Shropshire

Harry loved *free* running especially when I stayed with Julia and Peter in Ludlow and we would walk in Mortimer Forest and the Welsh Marches. There were other times when we would holiday at Windermere Manor Hotel at Windermere, in the Lake District, when it belonged to the Guide Dog Association. On these occasions we would join with other Guide Dog owners and their Guide Dogs on organised walks and outings in the area. Immediately on being set free, Harry would charge off, disappearing into the blue yonder, barking loudly as he ran. At first this used to concern me as he was reluctant to return on recall, finding it very difficult to tear himself away from exploring all those interesting smells.

Harry and I working on an audio guide of Clun Castle with Julia and Peter of the Dog Rose Trust

To overcome this situation however I used to turn around and walk back in the direction from whence we came. Harry was obviously keeping one eye on me because after a few minutes he would return to heel and I would feel a wet nose nudging my hand.

In the early days of free running in the forest Harry initially, unlike the Labradors and Labrador retriever crosses, never showed any interest in water, particularly that of the smelly and filthy kind. Imagine my surprise when walking in the Mortimer Forest near Ludlow with Harry running free, my friends turned to me and exclaimed, "We thought you said that Harry wasn't interested in water? Well that has just changed." I stopped and listened, I could hear splashing and my friends then described to me what was happening. Harry had found a drainage ditch which

Harry and I exploring Ludlow Castle with Julia and Maggie Galbarczyk

was about 80 yards long which contained about 6 inches of slimy mud and water. Harry was dashing up and down in this ditch getting himself filthy dirty and enjoying every minute of it, which was more than I did when cleaning him up in order to travel back in the car. From then on, Harry didn't miss an opportunity to sample the water.

The Guide Dog Association have been training and matching Guide Dogs to ensure compatibility with the varied and

In front of the chapel at Ludlow Castle with Julia and Maggie

often demanding occupations of the blind people whose lives they transform since 1940. A wealth of expertise has obviously been accumulated over this period. I always marvel how accurate this matching process is, in my own particular case near-perfect. No one however could have anticipated just how exceptional it was with Harry.

Harry and I had been together for 2 years when he developed an eye disease called *Pannus,* a disease of the cornea that Shepherds are very prone to. It is not curable but was successfully controlled with the use of eye drops. My blindness is total and I also have to have eye drops to regulate the eye pressures. Picture the scene: I apply my eye drops, upon which Harry comes and sits by my side and waits for my wife Jean to apply his eye drops. We both had one drop in each eye morning and night. Later I developed arthritis in my left hip; one month later Harry was diagnosed with arthritis in his hip so we both then started taking tablets for this. A few months after this, I underwent an operation on my back and two months later Harry, being an inquisitive dog, put his nose where he shouldn't and cut it. Harry then had to have an operation on his nose to have three stitches in it. I drew the line however when I had my hip replacement. Taking him on one side I told him, "You dare even think about it!"

Climbing over a stile with Nigel McDonald on a Shropshire country walk

I remember when Harry was diagnosed with the eye disease *Pannus*, the Ophthalmic consultant treating him remarked that in the USA dogs with this eye condition were often given shades to wear. With tongue in cheek he advised me to not even consider this. Imagine the scene, me walking down the busy high street wearing my shades being guided by Harry wearing his shades; it could certainly be a traffic stopper!

Harry kept me safe and on my toes and we walked on average three miles a day in town and open country and travelled on trains, taxis and buses. Harry was ten years old when he went to sleep for the last time. We had been together for eight exciting years during which we shared many adventures, made lots of friends, travelled widely and, thanks to Harry, safely. Harry's life, like Dorcas's, ended abruptly. He was due to retire and I had a retirement home all arranged for him with a friend who had a farm and lovely gardens. He had spent a few weekends with my friends, who he had come to know over the years, to see how he would settle. There were no problems: he loved it and Guide Dogs had checked it out and were happy with the arrangement.

I however had mixed feelings, happy that Harry would be able to relax and enjoy a well earned retirement in an environment which he obviously enjoyed, but I was going to miss him so very, very much. What a shock when he suddenly became ill and was diagnosed to have a tumour in his spleen. The vet performed an exploratory operation which revealed it to be inoperable. To save Harry further suffering and based on detailed discussions with the vet, who was so very supportive ensuring that Harry was comfortable and not suffering any pain, I made the decision for Harry to go to sleep providing I could be with him. Times like this are so very special and heart-rending with that trusting loving look in those deep brown eyes as I knelt on the floor with his head nestled into my lap as he gently drifted off to sleep. My daughter Nicola accompanied me and supported me throughout this difficult time which I really appreciated. Later, on reflection, I drew comfort from knowing that Harry was with me, with friends he knew and loved and had not gone to his new home when this happened.

Wills

Best friend number three: another male German Shepherd Guide Dog named Willis; I called him Wills and this was how people knew him. Wills was short haired, not as tall as Harry but the same weight with powerful shoulders and black and tan colouring with attractive markings. He was, like Harry, a macho personality but with a gentle nature. His most prominent feature, one which seemed to endear him to everyone was his head and face which was described to me to resemble a teddy bear. When I met Wills for the first time, prior to training, this head of his seemed to be very large and out of all proportion to the rest of his body which I eventually realised was due to him being ten pounds under weight, the rest of his body being very skinny in appearance. German Shepherds are a very sensitive breed and find it difficult to settle in kennels along with other dogs. This coupled with the policy of *bed and breakfasting* dogs in their final stages of training, with very often frequent changes in the volunteer families who were providing this service, accentuated the problem. In Wills' case this certainly appeared to be the situation because at first he would be very hesitant when eating his food, sometimes never eating it all. He seemed edgy and clingy as though he was thinking, "How long am I going to be with you?"

Within a few weeks of loving companionship in constant familiar surroundings however Wills began to regain weight, eating all his food and growing in confidence and within a couple of months had established himself as an integral member of our family.

The early weeks of our partnership were quite difficult and frustrating as I very quickly realised that Wills had a very strong personality. He represented a challenge for me: he was very determined and distracted by cats and dogs to the point where I nearly rejected him for the reasons I describe below. Based on my experience of living with dogs practically all my life and particularly with Dorcas and Harry, however gave me the gut feeling that once I had gained Wills' confidence and respect and established myself as the pack leader all that motivation and energy was going to help me and we were going to be a great partnership.

I did find a way of controlling Wills' distractions however when I realised that when he saw a cat or dog when he was in working mode he used to give himself away by lifting his tail and wagging it; this was accompanied by him making snorting noises rather like a horse. His tail used to brush under my hand which was holding the harness and of course I could hear the snorts whereupon I immediately told him to leave it, which he did. He never did realise that he gave the game away by this demeanour and eventually his behaviour modified and was controllable.

Wills was an attractive dog which was a bonus for me. As soon as I am on a train people start to talk to me. "What's your dog's name?" "How old is he?" "What does he eat?" and so on. The journey time passes quite quickly as I am engaged in conversation centring around Wills whilst he is quietly relaxed, stretched out on the floor of the carriage pretending to be asleep but with one ear cocked listening to the conversation.

The complete opposite occurs however when I travel without a Guide Dog using my white mobility cane. People seem to be embarrassed by the sight of a white cane; they don't know what to say so say nothing and because we are not able to see they think that we do not know that they are there. I will always remember a train journey to Liverpool boarding the train at Birmingham New Street rail station. The customer service man had put me on the train and into my seat assuring me that the train was bound for Liverpool. I waited for the train manager to confirm this just before we departed, but he didn't. The carriage had filled up, I could hear the passengers talking all around me, but when I asked them to confirm that this was indeed the Liverpool train, no one, but no one spoke; you could have heard a pin drop. After about fifteen minutes the train stopped, but no announcement was forthcoming from the train manager. To reassure myself I directed my voice towards where I had heard people talking asking them to confirm that this is Wolverhampton? No one answered, yet I knew that people were there and so it continued, no one speaking to me all the way to Liverpool.

With qualification over and Wills settling in to his new home it was time to choose his toys. Eventually we both settled on a solid rubber ring as being the most suitable, with a life of around four months. Wills took to his rubber ring almost immediately and it became an integral part of him, accompanying him everywhere that he went, carrying it in his mouth; he even took it into his basket when he settled down for the night, like a child's cuddly toy.

My voluntary work as a lecturer often involved me staying in hotels, with Wills of course. He quickly recognised my travel bag and soon I found his ring sitting next to it. Wills would watch me put it in an outside pouch of my bag and as soon as we arrived in the hotel bedroom he would sit with his nose within inches of the pouch, waiting for me to give it to him. I always had to remember to check that he didn't have it in his mouth when he was working in harness. I forgot on one occasion, only becoming aware when in the hotel lift another guest enquired what was that on the floor? You've guessed it, it was Wills' ring of course. Wills was very persistent with his ring, he would follow you every where, dropping it in front of your feet, in your lap, in your chair or just pushing it against your hand inviting you to play.

Sadly Wills developed arthritis in both his front legs which apparently followed difficulties experienced when he was in training. One possible cause being that his bone structure was not strong enough to absorb the shocks when pavement pounding. He was rested and received treatment at the time which seemed to cure the problem, but after four years working together and at the age of six years the problem reoccurred. During this time he never complained and was always keen and eager for work. I only realised that something

Wills with my friend Maurice Phillips holding his ring

was wrong when I began to feel through his harness handle what I can only describe as uneven walking when he was guiding me. Observation by the trainer and veterinary nurse at the Leamington centre confirmed that he was lame and arrangements were then made for him to see an animal orthopaedic specialist for diagnosis and treatment advice.

Sadly my worst fears were realised: his condition could only be stabilised not eradicated. In spite of the medication and extensive specialist treatment the decision was taken to retire him. Typical Wills though he made sure that people would remember him by ensuring that he was featured in a film for a TV programme and the GDBA had also featured us in a DVD, showing how he and Guide Dogs like him bring confidence and independence to blind people like me.

Then came for me one of the most difficult decisions and emotional experiences I have encountered with my four legged friends: should I keep him in his retirement or to let him be re-homed? In the best interests of Wills there could really be only one decision and that was to allow him to go to live with a loving family, who could give him the quality of life in his retirement that he so richly deserved. The couple that I chose, David and Irene, lived in the Chilterns in Buckinghamshire and their property was situated in two acres of grassland, which would be ideal for Wills with soft ground and no more hard pavements.

Guide Dogs have an excellent re-homing service, designed to organise in a sensitive way arrangements for this to happen and the Guide Dog owner is involved in every step of the procedure. So it was on March 9th 2009, Wills' seventh birthday, the day that Guide Dogs collected him to take him to his new home with David and Irene that our partnership was put on hold. This was a very emotional time for me; I had never before been in the position of saying goodbye knowing that I would never again feel that cold wet muzzle pushing into my hand or that warm, heavy body pushing so affectionately against my left leg whilst standing at the bus stop or in the train station, each of us reassuring the other that we cared.

This time my best friend was walking away from me, completely unaware that he would not be returning; how could I explain to him the situation? How would he feel after a couple of weeks into his new home? Would he miss me? Would he feel deserted? Would he settle and be happy? What a relief it was when Irene telephoned me a few days later to tell me that all was well. Wills had settled in his new home and had been busy exploring the two acres of garden, soft grass land, no more hard pavements to jar those leg joints.

My fourth and current Guide Dog is another German Shepherd, this time a female called Emma. When we were first introduced I thought she was a midget as she seemed so much smaller than my other dogs, but she still weighed 41 kilos. Emma was very attractive, just two years old, when we commenced training. Her coat is short, attractively marked and coloured, combining mixtures of black and tan, with creams of various densities. She has a typical German Shepherd face, tan coloured with slender, dark tan flecked with black muzzle which is cream on the underside, terminating in a black nose, big, brown attractive eyes and large pointed ears which are tan with black tips. A black saddle, tan legs and cream skirts completes the picture.

Emma's attractive appearance was very quickly confirmed by the number of people attempting to stroke and talk to her when I was standing in the bank or at bus stops. This distraction on the scale it occurred was something which I had not experienced with my other dogs as the general impression the public have in their minds of German Shepherds is that they are aggressive, guard type dogs, so their approach to my other dogs was rather cautious. Emma's attractive appearance however seemed to overcome that fear. Other characteristics were, her long tail which trailed the ground by about a quarter of an inch and her habit of licking my hands at every opportunity; I call her a *lick dog* because of this.

Emma, however, very nearly didn't make it to be a Guide Dog due to her suffering from *atopic dermatitis*. This is a most common dermatological form of skin allergy in dogs which is caused by sensitivity to substances in the environment; in Emma's case she is sensitive to house dust mites, grass and weed pollens. The problem is obviously prevalent during the summer months, but can be controlled with medication and use of antiseptic wipes plus regular visits to the vet. The effect such an allergy has on the dog's behaviour and work, plus the ability and willingness of the Guide Dog owner to cope and take responsibility for maintaining the dog in good health, becomes a major concern when matching the Guide Dog with its potential owner. Having experienced various health problems with my previous dogs, and my affinity with German Shepherds, I was given the opportunity to train with Emma and having been introduced to her I had that gut feel that she was going to be a good friend to me and well worth the extra effort which has proved to be the case.

My experience with my other dogs led me to believe that, unlike Labradors, they were not food scavengers; obviously if food was left exposed and accessible they would not resist the temptation to explore and taste. Maybe I was the lucky one because my dogs did not immediately go searching the room or investigating litter bins whenever they were off the lead in unfamiliar situations. The practice learnt in training of always being aware of the temptation that dogs have of scavenging, and people tempting dogs with titbits when in public places, needs reinforcing at all times. When temptation occurs, it is necessary to consistently reprimand the dog so that it realises that it just isn't worth it, always however remembering to praise it when it ignores the temptation.

I remember a situation which occurred when giving a Guide Dog talk at a coffee morning with Dorcas, my first Guide Dog. I was in the middle of my presentation when a lady interrupted me to enquire if my dog liked biscuits. I explained that she was not allowed biscuits other than dog biscuits and had been taught to resist the temptation to steal. "Why do you ask?" I enquired. "Well", the lady replied, "Dorcas has been looking at a biscuit which has dropped on the floor just a few inches from her nose but has not tried to eat it." I immediately removed the biscuit and made a big fuss of her and at the same time praising her for resisting the temptation. I couldn't have wished for a better example of how well trained Guide Dogs are and I felt very proud of Dorcas that day.

Emma is proving to be the exception however; given the opportunity she is always in the kitchen when food is around, something which had to be immediately corrected due to the trip hazard which she presented. She used to sit next to me at the dining table at meal times putting her nose up near my plate which led me to believe that at some time she had been given food scraps and therefore was always waiting for that tasty morsel to come her way. When training on walks Emma exhibited the same interest in scavenging; initially she would make slight diversions to investigate anything found on the pavement which might be tasty and, if I was not quick enough, eat it.

With the guidance of Tony, her trainer, we were able to control and deter this habit. Tony would collect some bread crusts from my home before we started our walk and then go some way ahead scattering crusts on the way. I would follow and if Emma should try to deviate to the scraps I would severely reprimand her and praise her when she responded to my correction. Incidentally Tony retrieved the untouched scraps of bread on conclusion of the exercise. I am pleased to report after twelve months or so of maintaining and reinforcing this training she has realised that scavenging is a waste of time.

One must, however, always be aware of the dog's vulnerability when in public. An example of this occurred when I visited my local bank, an incident which made me both angry with myself for not realising what was happening and with the lady perpetrator for doing what she did, in spite of the flash on Emma's lead advising *Please do not feed me* and on her harness *Please do not distract me I am working*. The incident happened whilst my attention was distracted during conducting a transaction with the cashier. A lady standing in the queue behind me tapped me on the shoulder and said, "I think you ought to know that a lady has just come up to your dog and given her what looked to be a biscuit," which Emma had apparently eaten. The lady in question had then disappeared leaving me unable to complain and worrying was it really a biscuit or something else? I have been lucky in the past as so far as I am aware my other dogs would sniff it, but refuse it in this situation.

My training with Emma was all conducted from my home (domiciliary training) which I preferred as it meant that we were both training on the routes that I would be using every day and having had three Guide Dogs previously it was felt that I was familiar with the basics. Emma was quick to settle into her new home and quickly responded to the treats (food pellets) system of incentive rewards when accomplishing the different tasks requested. One task was to find the operating button which is set into the box on the pedestrian crossing pole. This exercise was particularly difficult for me: and I always had difficulty in finding the pole, never mind the operating button. To overcome this Emma was taught

Emma

to indicate the operating button box with her nose whilst at the same time I had a treat in my hand. So when I pressed the button I opened my hand allowing the treat to fall into the waiting open mouth. I am sure that Emma thinks that those boxes all contain her treats and consequently I find the control button every time.

Initially like my other dogs, with the exception of Dorcas, Emma was cat and dog distracted. It took a little time to get the message across that she didn't divert to talk to other dogs when she was working in harness; if I suffered a lapse in concentration however she was quick to take advantage.

I use public transport quite a lot, particularly the trains. Coventry rail station is managed by Virgin who give excellent customer service, *Journey Care,* with friendly staff. This service includes being able to reserve my seat in advance and when I tell them that I will be travelling with my Guide Dog they reserve two seats next to each other, one being for my Guide Dog, who obviously does not use the seat, but the floor space provided by the seat.

Emma, in keeping with all my Guide Dogs has been quick to settle in to new surroundings; when I stay with my friends she sleeps overnight in their study and once I have settled her we don't hear a peep from her. When I stayed in hotels, which was quite frequent due to my work as a public speaker, she also settled down quite quickly in the room and could be left quite happily on her own on the occasions when I choose not to take her into the restaurant.

Schools presentations, particularly the ones which I give to primary schools, I make very interactive. I talk the children through a day in my life, a blind person's life, from when I wake up in a morning to when I go to bed at night. This is really a disability awareness presentation. I describe and demonstrate, with the children's help, how I am able to do things that the children possibly take for granted, never thinking how difficult those things would be to do if they were like me and couldn't see to do them.

A real test for Emma's obedience is when I am showing the children how to guide a blind person when they are walking in the street. Having demonstrated to the children how Emma guides me when working in harness, I take my mobility cane and demonstrate how a blind person who doesn't have a Guide Dog uses it to aid their mobility. When I invite a child to come out to the front of the group and guide me around imaginary obstacles, Emma who has been lying down remaining quiet and still, immediately on seeing me with my mobility cane puts her head up and with ears pricked follows my every movement. On seeing the child guiding me Emma immediately sits up and it is as though she is registering her concern, "Hey that's my job. Can I really trust those children to guide Eric safely?" Sometimes she will start to leave her position and come towards me to take over, but responds immediately when I tell her to go back and sit, which always impresses the audience. It is also interesting how on the odd occasion when I am not able to take Emma with me she will, on seeing me get out my mobility cane, immediately go and sit in her basket with her ears down and that look, "I don't think much of this, why can't I come?"

I really do enjoy talking to Primary school children (6-11 year olds). When question time comes along at the end of the presentation they are always eager to ask me questions. I always preface this period by telling them that I don't mind how personal their questions are. As soon as a question enters their heads out it pops; very often teachers tell me afterwards that they were pleased that little Joe asked that question, they were dying to ask it but didn't have the courage. Children also have some novel ideas on how a Guide Dog can help a blind person. Once I asked the children in an assembly if they thought that I could ride a bike; in fact I used to enjoy cycling but on a tandem. One little boy, aged about 8, put up his hand and when asked he replied, "Yes I think you could. You could fix a side car to your bike, have your Guide Dog sitting in it and she could tell you where to go." I could just imagine Emma sitting in that side car dressed in leather helmet and goggles with a scarf around her neck billowing out in the slipstream.

Obedience training: from experience gained with my other dogs I have realised how valuable play obedience training can be. Every day I play with Emma and these play times are also obedience reminders, which she seems to enjoy, always coming back for more, retrieving her *Kong* whether I have thrown it or hidden it (seldom in the same place twice). When she is exceptionally good I reward her with a treat (a pellet of her normal food). During our playing we do a lot of sits, up-sits, downs, wait and stay commands. It is a rewarding feeling when she has been waiting some distance away in the sit or down position for me to call her to heel, then when I hear her coming I put my hand up and tell her to wait and sit which she does, then after a pause tell her to come to heel which she does. This level of obedience gains her a big hug and more treats from me.

This play obedience pays off because when I am in an unfamiliar area or an area with lots of distractions, especially if she is free running, I am confident that she will respond to my commands. On returning to me she always presses her wet nose into my hand as if to say, "I am here". We participate in this obedience play training every day; sometimes it is only for a few minutes with a couple of commands and other times it can be twenty minutes or more. Following a long session I play with her, getting her ball on a rope and we play tugging it; it's important to remember to let her win a few times!

Like my other dogs Emma is quick to learn new routes; show her once and she will nearly always find it a second time and definitely on the third attempt. On new routes where I am also finding my way, she seems to be able to read my mind and sometimes pre-empt my next move, always being very quick to respond to my commands in these situations. I have to be aware however that on the odd occasion Emma can anticipate my next command incorrectly and when this happens she is very persistent; it is me that's made the mistake, not her, or is there something interesting in this new direction?

Emma is a caring dog; when she is free, not working in harness or on a lead, she will quite frequently come to me and poke her nose into my hand thus reassuring me that she is around. I find this an endearing feature in her character that she should think this way. Emma does this particularly if I am with a group of friends who at the same time are talking and playing with her; she will frequently break off and return to me poking her nose into my hand as if to seek reassurance for herself and to tell me "It's OK, I am still here and behaving myself."

CHAPTER 10

EXPLORING CATHEDRALS

Cathedrals are beautiful, majestic buildings, for those of you who are sighted; a pleasure to the eye, history handed down from generation to generation, an atmosphere of peace, the focal point for prayer for so many pilgrims throughout the ages. You stand and gaze in wonder and awe, pondering on this feat of construction which has stood the test of time. Maybe you have travelled to this Cathedral from afar and when you turned a corner in the road or topped the brow of a hill, suddenly there on the horizon you became aware of this magnificent building, standing there dominating the countryside for miles around, surveying and beckoning. Perhaps you came upon it unexpectedly, you

Worcester Cathedral

Exploring the model in a Touch and Hearing centre

turned a corner in the street and there it was, suddenly filling your whole field of vision.

But if you are visually impaired you don't get this grand vista; you can't see the beautiful Rose window, the fan vaulting with its fine stone tracery, the carved wooden screens or delicate wrought iron work. And how do I find out about details such as the shape and size of the building itself, the flying buttresses, the medieval bosses on the roof, the colour of the stonework? Does it have a tower or a spire? What kind of building is this in which we are standing? The experience of visually impaired people in this situation only serves to heighten their sense of loss, but on the positive side it generates a feeling of mystery, one which has to be challenged and explored.

My explorations of such buildings started with the use of *The Touch and Hearing Centres*, a research project devised by Professor John Hull of Birmingham University, who is himself blind. The first of these centres was installed in Coventry Cathedral in 1986. Coventry is where I have lived since 1973 and the Provost of Coventry Cathedral, the Very Rev. John F Petty had become a friend of mine through our mutual interest in tandem riding. He was the person responsible for introducing me to the Birmingham University research team, a relationship which developed into me becoming an active Associate member, on a voluntary basis.

My role as an associate tended to be that of assisting with the initial physical surveys of the Cathedral and acting as a sounding board for ideas and the final product. Another function that I was sometimes called upon to fill was that of assisting in the marketing of the project to Cathedral Friends organisations who were often responsible for providing the money for the centres. One such memorable occasion was when, in this connection, I delivered my presentation from the pulpit of Chichester Cathedral, speaking to the Friends of that Cathedral.

Raising awareness of the work of the project, both with the public and with those organisations concerned with opening up their buildings by providing access to visually impaired people was something else with which I became involved. An example of this was when I presented a paper on behalf of Professor Hull at an International Conference held at Strathclyde University, Glasgow in 1990 when Glasgow was the European City of Culture.

Since becoming blind, and up until the time I became involved in the *Cathedrals through the Touch and Hearing* project, I had rarely visited Cathedrals and when I did it was always on the arm of a sighted friend. I remember listening to my friend's interpretation of the building, receiving the information second-hand so to speak. It was their idea of what they thought my interests would be, but very often it reflected only their own.

I listen dutifully, struggling to build a mental picture from all those enthusiastic descriptions of all these wonderful things around me, when, suddenly my finger would be grabbed and placed down hard on something which felt, cold, rough and dirty and at the same time I would hear my friend's excited voice exclaiming, "Isn't it wonderful, isn't it marvellous? It's a carving in the stone work of a little mouse and it's just peeping out from behind some ears of corn." I am sorry, but to me it's not a bit exciting, it feels horrible, but it however proves the point, which is that something which has been designed and produced to be very attractive to the eye can be just the opposite to a visually impaired person.

To communicate a Cathedral in all its glory to a visually impaired person, as they, a sighted person, perceives it, is a mistake. The sighted person doing the guiding, needs to stop and consider the world of the visually impaired person. For instance when a sighted person enters a Cathedral, there in an instant, is the whole panorama of the Cathedral's interior exposed to you - its size, its complexity, the colours and its glory. When I as a visually impaired person walk through that door I see nothing. I have to build my picture in my mind, block by block and I do this by using my other senses, those of touch hearing and smell.

CATHEDRALS THROUGH TOUCH AND HEARING

Professor Hull, being blind himself, developed his research project, *Cathedrals Through Touch and Hearing* which Birmingham University funded, with this in mind. The system was developed using 3 basic components, housed in a unit called a *Touch and Hearing Centre*.

First was a solid scale wooden model of the Cathedral specifically designed and made for tactile purposes. This model is completely different in principle from the usual type of models normally to be found enclosed in glass cases for sighted people to see. This model is a simplified version; it is not a facsimile but is a simplified, symbolic interpretation. The intention is that it should represent the equivalent of what a sighted person receives from a first glance. With that single glance a sighted person fundamentally knows what size and shape the building is together with its complexity and can also form an impression of what they expect to see inside. This model therefore is designed to provide that equivalent. I remember placing my hands on the model of Lichfield Cathedral and feeling the three spires: how large, tall and slender they were and I found myself comparing them with the tall, slender contemporary design of the cross on the roof of Coventry's new Cathedral and then of course the square towers of Worcester, Gloucester and Hereford Cathedrals.

Then I discovered that little box on the side of the model which was a representative model of a typical suburban dwelling house. It was like the one in which I live and produced in the same scale as the Cathedral model. Then I was told that if I were to place 5 of these houses on top of each other they would all fit into the nave of this Cathedral; that's an incredible thought, an experience which gives one a real feeling of the size of this beautiful building.

At the side of the model, mounted on the same base board, is a 3-dimensional elevated floor plan cut in wood of a contrasting colour from that of the base. This contrast in colour assists those with partial sight to detect the plan's outline. The visually impaired person sits down in front of this plan which, together with the model, is housed in a purpose-built cabinet. The materials used in the construction of this cabinet, part Perspex and wood, have been specially selected in order that they blend within the environment in which the cabinet is sited.

Edward Kelsey (Ted) recording the commentary for Winchester Cathedral using a binaural microphone. Note the hat on the dummy head.

The visually impaired visitor sat in front of the plan and model and accessed a cassette player which is controlled by foot pedals. Through the head set the visitor received a specially prepared audio description of the building and plan using the model over which one's fingers are directed. A point to note here: so much of our language is dependent upon the assumption that we are all sighted that to write for the fingers and not the eyes becomes a fascinating and subtle art. Braille and large print versions of the audio description are also available.

Exploring a large column during a recording session

The audio tour of the Cathedral ran for approximately 10 minutes and provided a fundamental description of the building. This brief description, along with the tactile exploration of both model and plan, really only provide a snapshot of the Cathedral, which is fine if the visitor only has a limited amount of time available.

In order to derive maximum benefit from this facility however the visually impaired visitor was strongly recommended to use the third component of the project - The *Acoustic Fingerprint Guide*, developed by Dog Rose Sound of Ludlow, specialists in this field. This was no ordinary audio guide but one which had been specially developed and recorded in the individual locations, to which reference is made. The audio recording is not merely a sound documentary of the radio type, but is a recorded f*ingerprint* of the space. The sounds we experience vary according to that space, such as bells, organs, clapping of hands, voices singing, foot steps, background noises, the curious way when you move from a Lady Chapel through the choir into the nave and then down into the crypt, all seek to confirm this.

I feel that I have been fortunate living in Coventry as I have been able to experience its wonderful modern Cathedral when and as often as I wished and that has been many, many times. It is this Cathedral that really opened up my mind to the possibilities that exist to enable people like me to explore and enjoy the history, spirituality and craftsmanship which buildings like Cathedrals have to offer: this proves 'Beauty is not just in the eyes of the beholder, but also in the fingers, ears and noses'.

Coventry's new Cathedral is a wonderfully tactile building. Many different materials were used in its construction such as stone, concrete, marble, porcelain, wood, glass and metals; these are combined with the differing textures, both natural and manmade. Together with the sound made when they are tapped, they provide all the clues for the budding detectives amongst us.

The more I use my fingers to explore the more accurate I become at recognising the various materials. After feeling a marble column for instance, I realised why my grandmother had a marble slab in her pantry; marble is a very dense and cold material which is ideal for keeping fish and meat fresh.

We are very fortunate in the West Midlands, in that we have three Cathedrals which are so very different, the medieval Lichfield, the contemporary Coventry and the early eighteenth century Birmingham. Each of these structures feels quite different and each has a different characteristic space. Not too far away we have the Cathedrals of Gloucester, Hereford and Worcester, all very imposing structures and all willing to yield their history and secrets to the probing finger tips, sensitive ears and noses of visually impaired people.

Lichfield Cathedral

I well remember Worcester as it is my home town. I can see it now in my mind, in that famous setting, with its imposing west window looking out over the River Severn and the county cricket ground. I remember visiting it so many times when I was younger, sometimes with my mother and grandmother. My favourite part of the Cathedral then was the tomb of King John, I would stand gazing at it, imagining what he must have been like and thinking of the Magna Carta. Yet the Worcester

chapter ten

Cathedral which I visit now as a blind person is a different one and in a way a more interesting one. I am much more aware of the feeling of space and the smells of age: tapestries and old flags mingle with the scent of fresh flowers and the dull roar of the city traffic outside is lost when you step into the musty smelling crypt or walk in the fresh air of the cloisters.

Returning to the *Touch and Hearing Centres*, the wooden scale models were produced from various woods; lime was chosen as the standard, which I like the feel of: I have come to enjoy the feeling of wood. It's a natural material, pleasant to touch, a living material, warm and strong. One is able to feel the grain in the wood when you run your fingers over the model tracing its shapes and dimensions, helping you to form that picture of the building in your mind.

I remember running my fingers over the model of Lincoln Cathedral and getting a surprise. I had visited that Cathedral when I was sighted, even staying in the hotel opposite on many occasions during my frequent business trips into the area so I still hold a clear picture of it in my mind. But what I hadn't realised was the size of the area it covered and how complex the building was with its many flying buttresses. The scale model revealed all of this to me because I was getting a bird's eye view of it and I found it fascinating.

Sitting in front of the centre, my fingers, having been guided over the wooden model of the building by the audio commentary, were now being directed to explore the 3-dimensional floor plan alongside. Immediately I was able to locate my position within the building and working from there my fingers were guided through doors, various chapels, along the nave and into the transept, through the choir and into the

Lady Chapel, stopping on the way to listen to various interesting facts relating to that particular position within the building.

I made mental notes of the parts of the building and artefacts which interested me or caught my imagination so that I could study them when I explored the building afterwards. The brief synopsis of the building's history together with some of the more technical details included in the audio commentary helped me to get a feeling for it and the events which had shaped it into the building we have today.

Discovering the Cathedrals through these *Touch and Hearing Centres* and now particularly the improved interactive centres developed by Dog Rose Sound, whets the appetite for more exploration.

EXPERIENCING COVENTRY CATHEDRAL THROUGH THE SENSES

Listening to the *Acoustic Fingerprint Guide* reveals the many sensual experiences which Coventry Cathedral has to offer. The guide starts with a recording of the Cathedral bells, followed by an introduction. The sound quality of the recording is impressive. I remember listening to the Coventry Cathedral guide introduction, having taken a seat at the rear of the nave as suggested. Suddenly I hear the voice of the Provost of the Cathedral, the Very Rev. John F Petty, who you will recall is a friend of mine, welcoming me to the Cathedral of St. Michael. I am caught off balance for a moment or two because I am convinced that he is actually sitting alongside me talking to me, such is the quality of the sound. The guide then takes me on a tour of the Cathedral, stopping at places of special interest, where the story of that place will be told and where possible things to touch will be suggested.

A special concession granted to us visually impaired folk which the guide alerts us to, is that we are able to gain access to areas in the Cathedral not normally available to the public, in order that we may have tactile experiences of a particular item or section of the building.

Of my early tactile experiences, I will always remember the feelings which I experienced when I touched the unusual sandstone font in Coventry Cathedral. It is a huge weathered boulder weighing approximately 3 tons and yet is set into its marble plinth on a single slender stem of bronze. The top is hollowed out in the shape of a scallop shell, but otherwise it is untouched and as it stood for centuries near the road in a valley near Bethlehem. I stood with my fingers resting on its rough surface and imagined that our Lord Jesus, over 2000 years ago, could well have touched, or rested his body against this very stone on which my fingers now lay.

A completely different experience, in tactile terms, is provided by the famous Baptistry window, designed by John Piper, which is located behind the font. The guide describes this window, which is larger than the great East window in Gloucester Cathedral, in detail. It occupies the full 80 feet height of the wall and gently curves out across its width of 40 feet. The window is made up of many rectangular panels of stained glass separated by stone mullions and transoms. I discovered that the stained glass is set back from the front of the mullion, which is square edged and broadens out as it recedes towards the glass panel, the recess being about the depth of my forearm. With my fingers I can trace the individual, irregular shaped pieces of glass, which are set in lead; the surface of the glass feels coarse and the shapes like jagged rectangles, except for the first and last vertical rows which are circles or discs; the audio guide explains this is an echo of the thirteenth century when it was a favourite device of the early glass designers. The window viewed as a whole resembles, I imagine, a huge chequer board in the way that the mullions and transoms divide up the window.

The pillars, or columns, in a Cathedral fascinate me as they are very tactile. I like to put my arms around them and hug them to get a feel for their size, shape and complexity. I can tell if they are square in shape or circular, maybe fluted or very often

Exploring the carved capital of a column

a combination of both. As I run my fingers lightly over the stonework I can feel the mason's chisel marks, the grain of the stone together with its temperature. Cotswold stone is warmer to the touch than for instance York and certainly marble. They provide me with all sorts of clues which assist in determining the building's age and history. The stonework in the older Cathedrals is dusty and flaky to the touch whereas in the new modern Cathedrals like Coventry it is clean and smooth.

I am always making comparisons: the long slender star-shaped columns of Coventry Cathedral moulded in concrete have a very fine, smooth surface finish - no mason's chisel marks here - achieved through the use of a very fine stone aggregate, methinks, with some marble for its finishing layer; the surface is mirrored by the exceptional finish on the column formers. The columns here are formed by pouring concrete into a mould compared with the conventional method of carving them from solid stone by masons using chisels and stone carving tools. These pillars which hold up the vaulted wooden ceiling are comparatively slender, with their star shapes tapering inwards right down to the floor.

A little game I love playing when I hear sighted visitors around is to run my fingers down the column towards the floor where at its base, just a few inches above the floor, I feel the supporting bronze shoe with its incredibly small bronze pin under the base of the pillar. Sliding my hand under the base of the pillar, between the shoe and the floor, with my fingers divided around the supporting pin, it looks as if the pillar is sitting in the palm of my hand and I am holding it up. This evidently produces a few glances of astonishment and questions of how can this be possible.

I have hugged and caressed many, many columns to date but of all these, two Cathedrals remain in my memory. Coventry Cathedral for the reasons just described and in complete contrast the magnificent Durham Cathedral built in a very different age of design, materials and building techniques. In Durham Cathedral the huge columns are circular in shape, with a spiral groove cut into each column radiating from top to bottom. The unusual design created by this spiral groove is further enhanced by each column having a bead, or beads, of various shapes laid within the groove which serves to partly fill the groove, making each column an individual one. The overall effect conveyed by these columns was one of massive strength which is further enhanced by their shortness, due to the comparatively low roof: here the stonework feels quite dusty and crumbly.

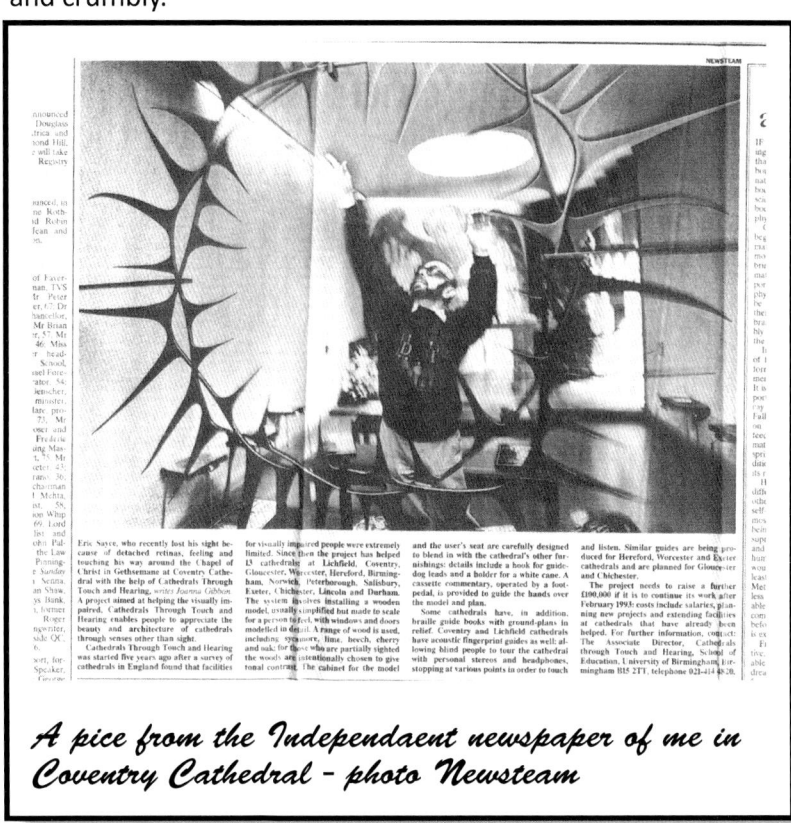

A pice from the Independaent newspaper of me in Coventry Cathedral - photo Newsteam

chapter ten

An aritlcle in the national newspaper *The Independent* described the many different ways by which I, a visually impaired person, explored Cathedrals. *The Independent*'s reporter interviewed me during tours of both Coventry and Gloucester Cathedrals, which had been arranged for the occasion. The article was based on my experiences gained during these tours. Dorcas, my Guide Dog, accompanied me on both. She has become so familiar with the route inside Coventry Cathedral that she now automatically stops at all the places of tactile interest. She also provided good photo opportunities which were not lost on the accompanying photographer.

My early visits to Cathedrals seemed to raise a great deal of public interest, particularly in the media. In addition to the articles printed in both national and local newspapers I have been interviewed by the late John Dunn on BBC Radio 2's *John Dunn Show*, the BBC World Radio Service broadcast an interview with me, plus the local radio stations such as BBC-WM, BBC-CWR and local talking newspapers, all of which serve to increase the awareness of this facility in the minds of both sighted and visually impaired people.

The acoustics in a building vary greatly and one becomes very aware of the changes in this respect which help to identify the different areas. Coventry Cathedral has many good examples of this: for instance when one walks down the nave from the glass panelled West end, the quality of the sound changes. At first it's clear and resonant, sharp and large but then it becomes duller and softer as one approaches the chancel and high altar. To reach the Chapel of Industry, one passes through a narrow passageway where the sound closes in due to the confined space. Then suddenly, as one enters the Chapel of Industry itself one experiences a sudden loud volume of *bright* sound, echoing and reverberating around this circular glass walled building with its very high ceiling. The Chapel is built like a chapter house in the much older Cathedrals. It is attached to the main building and projecting towards the street, from whence most of the sound comes.

I then leave the Chapel of Industry and walk towards the high altar; as I re-enter the passageway, the acoustics change again. I stop outside the tiny Chapel of Christ in Gethsemane where the wrought iron screen of the Crown of Thorns separates the chapel from the aisle. I stand and listen, fingering the screen; as I do so immediately I am aware of a feeling of peace, a wrap-around quietness produced by the very small confines of this chapel. Standing quite close to the screen, I become aware of the screen and the resonating sounds around me on the outside of the chapel, acting as a barrier against the sounds trying to penetrate its peace. I tap the screen a few times with my finger and immediately a deep clanging sound reverberates all around the screen, a sound completely different from all the others which I have experienced.

The *Crown of Thorns* wrought iron screen, designed by Sir Basil Spence, the Architect of the Cathedral, was made by the apprentices of the Royal Engineers at Chatham and given by them as a gift to the Cathedral. To me the screen feels like a good example of modern contemporary design, symbolic in nature. It is made in the shape of a crown of thorns in two dimensions. I feel how the inner circle has smaller thorns, all similar, triangular in shape, all projecting inwards, whilst the longer crowns on the outside of the crown are more irregular. I find that the points of these thorns, like the real thing, are quite sharp; the two strands intertwine in twelve places.

During my visit to Chichester Cathedral, when I addressed the Friends of the Cathedral, I was fortunate to meet the Commanding Officer of the Royal Engineers at the time the screen was made. He, being retired but aware of my love of Coventry Cathedral, asked me if I had found the apprentices' badge which they had placed on the screen as a sign of their craftsmanship. I had to confess that I hadn't and was not aware of it. I have subsequently discovered it, having been given its location by the C.O., but that I will leave for you to explore and find; suffice to say that the mark is a repetition of their epaulette badge, the shape of a grenade with the initials set within it. This mark evidently was the idea of Sir Basil Spence who after having inspected and approved of the work of the apprentices suggested to the C.O. that in the same way as the stone masons and carpenters traditionally left their signature or mark as a sign of ownership to the work that they produce, then the apprentice engineers should do the same.

I cannot leave Coventry Cathedral without mentioning the world- famous Graham Sutherland tapestry which shows the seated figure of Christ with hands raised in compassion. The tapestry, which covers the complete wall and hangs from ceiling to floor, replaces the usual stained glass East window. The woollen tapestry was woven in France, on the longest loom in the world which is over 500 years old. Although the Cathedral vergers have a tapestry book which contains a sample of the tapestry for visitors to feel, I was fortunate to touch the real thing and was surprised to find that it felt very firm and hard to the touch rather like a cord carpet.

Gloucester Cathedral

Cathedrals are all different and one develops special memories of individual ones visited. Gloucester Cathedral is another of my favourites and I remember Abbot Seabrook's Chantry Chapel which one approaches through a narrow entrance. The acoustic effect of the screen around this small chapel is that it cuts off the reverberation from the nave and gives it a sense of isolation and appropriate quietness. The effigy of Abbot Seabrook lying on top of his tomb chest is quite interesting in a tactile sense, but it is something else which I remember as it gave me great pleasure to explore. What is it? It is a small modern wooden statue of St. Peter, patron saint of the Cathedral, situated on a pedestal at shoulder height to the left of the tomb. As I run my fingers over the statue, I can feel the large keys which he is holding in his right hand and the open book in his left. Around the base of the statue and at his feet I can make out the tiny square mesh of a fishing net and also trace the outline of some little fish with the tip of my finger, which reminds me that he was once a fisherman. The feel of the natural wood carving is pleasant to the touch.

The other area in this Cathedral I remember with interest is the 15th century Lady Chapel, dedicated to the Virgin Mary, which is the largest in the country. The reason I remember it however is not due to its size or its great East Window, but because of 3 of the tombs which it contains.

One is of Bishop Miles Smith, one of the translators of the authorised version of the Bible, which is sited in the centre of the chapel. The other two are of his two daughters, Elizabeth *chapter ten*

Williams, who died in 1622 at the age of 17 and Marjorie Clent, her sister; both daughters died in childbirth. I found the alabaster effigy of Elizabeth particularly poignant; she is lying propped up on her elbow facing her father with the little baby wrapped in swaddling clothes beside her. I trace the shape of the baby's clothes with my fingers and then move my fingers up to the effigy of Elizabeth. I feel the shape of her head and the cap she is wearing. Then moving my fingers down to her neck to the ruff around her neck and the top of her delicate long flowing dress with inset bodice panel of fine lace with lots of small buttons forming a V shaped pattern down its front. These small buttons also adorn the sleeves which have deep cuffs and I discover that she is holding a prayer book in her left hand. My fingers continue to follow the flow of the dress towards her feet and then a surprise. She is wearing high heeled shoes. I didn't

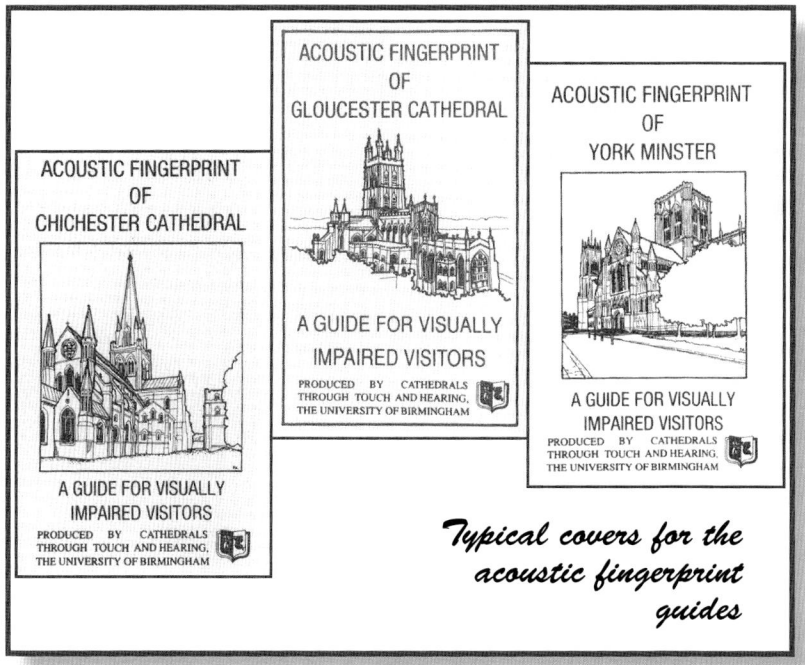

Typical covers for the acoustic fingerprint guides

expect this as I thought that people wore flat wooden sandal type shoes, and now I found that the fashion for ladies' high heeled shoes commenced around this time, the 1620s.

I remember thinking to myself that lots of people visit this Lady Chapel, read the information on the small cards placed beside the tombs and upon realising the sad circumstances surrounding the death of these young girls, think to themselves, "Oh what a shame," and probably miss completely the fact that they are wearing high heeled shoes. An example of how we visually impaired people, through having to fine-tune our other senses, very often become much more aware of details, which are often overlooked by our sighted friends.

I find that being forced to use my other senses enables me to rediscover Cathedrals and although I sometimes wish that I could see the artefacts and buildings that I feel, to see if they look as interesting and beautiful as the impression which I form in my mind. Writing this however has made me stop and think and I am realising that my senses have developed in such a way that, based on my memory of the sighted world, I am now able to build pictures and impressions of the solid physical elements that I come into contact with, without that painful sense of loss. This is not true however of my feelings where people who I love, my family, my grandchildren, my Guide Dogs and my friends who are close to me, are concerned. My feelings of loss in this respect are still at times very painful.

Note:
In 1988 John Hull initiated *Cathedrals Through Touch and Hearing*, a scheme which has provided 17 English cathedrals with wooden models and elevated ground plans for the

benefit of blind visitors. The *Cathedrals Through Touch and Hearing* project has now finished and not all of the Cathedrals have their models on display. Because changes have taken place in many of the Cathedrals the *Acoustic Fingerprint Guides* are not always available. However, many of them can be listened to on the Dog Rose Trust's website, Dog Rose Sound:
www.dogrosesound.org

Chapter 11

The Vista Story

My serious interest in tandems and tandem riding all started when I was involved in raising funds in order to provide equipment for the local Resource Centre for the Blind in Coventry. The patron of our fund-raising project was the Very Reverend John Petty, Provost of Coventry Cathedral, himself a keen cyclist.

Setting off on a ride with me as the stoker

It all started when I and a fellow blind fund-raising colleague, Jeanette, were having a quiet chat, swapping ideas at a Christmas party for the blind and partially sighted children of the *Peepers Club*. Little did we think then that we were about to embark on an idea that would bring a better quality of life and an increase in both confidence and independence, to say nothing of the improvement in the social lives of we blind and partially sighted people.

I had met the Provost about 12 months previously when the BBC were filming a programme for television called *My City.* Someone had told them about a club which I had helped to found called the *Peepers*, whose principle objective was to introduce and encourage blind and partially sighted adults and children to sample a wide range of sporting and leisure activities. These activities included archery, which was my particular interest at the time and goal ball the interest of my friend and fellow founder member, Derek Allan.

Derek had recently taken part in a tandem marathon race for visually impaired participants in Spalding, Lincolnshire. In fact when the other participants heard that our club did not have a tandem of our own they organised a whip round amongst themselves to start us on our way to procuring one, which we eventually did. Panic! Panic! When the BBC contacted us we had only just acquired it and did not have a *pilot* - that's the able-bodied person who rides on the front and steers and controls it - and as often happens when you are not prepared, the BBC wanted to film us riding it.

I racked my brains and then remembered a friend telling me that the Bishop of Coventry, together with the Provost, had ridden a tandem around the Diocese recently raising money for the church urban aid fund. Would they help us? I wondered. I didn't know either of them and riding with a blind person, for you able-bodied folk, well it's a little unusual isn't it? I gathered up my courage and telephoned; after all nothing ventured, nothing gained. The Provost answered and yes he would be pleased to help us and the necessary arrangements were made there and then. No time for practice, however, as the BBC wanted to film us on the following Saturday morning.

Saturday morning duly arrived, so did the BBC's film crew, just at the same time as the Provost. There was no time for introductions so the Provost checked the tandem over and made the necessary adjustments while the film crew were telling us what to do, where they wanted us to ride and so on.

Then we were off, the Provost riding as *pilot* and me acting as *stoker* riding on the back. We rode out of the Sports Centre with more than a wobble or two and turned right onto the quiet road outside. Well, it was usually quiet, but what was that I could hear close behind us? It was a juggernaut, of all things. I started to feel a little nervous but was then reassured as the Provost was an experienced tandem rider. As the juggernaut eventually squeezed past us breathing fire and feeling very menacing, apprehension changed to relief.

There were no further incidents with the exception of the occasional wobble or two as the film crew completed their work getting us to ride past, turn and turn about with the obligatory smiles and hand waving. Having completed the ride, the Provost and I alighted from the tandem and proceeded into the coffee bar to have a well-earned cuppa. It was then and only then that I confessed to the Provost that I had been very reassured during the incident with the juggernaut; it was a great relief having an experienced *Pilot* controlling matters on the front, as this was the first time I had ridden on a tandem. Imagine my feelings when the Provost turned to me and replied, "Didn't I tell you, this was the first time that I have ridden *pilot* as I am usually the *stoker*.

Our partnership occasion has since developed into friendship and the sharing of many cycling experiences together. The major ones were riding together in the Spalding marathon, a serious competitive race and of course the Coventry Tandem Team marathons, which we developed together. One year the Provost was invited to conduct the annual National Cyclists' Memorial Service at the war memorial on the green in Meriden.

All these activities served to raise public awareness of the fact that we blind and partially sighted people can, and do, given the right training and motivation, indulge ourselves in sporting and leisure activities, with confidence and safety – blindness need not be a barrier.

We had this idea that was going to have such an impact - the Coventry Tandem Team Marathon. It was one of those throw-away ideas; someone said, "Hey what if we could close one side of the Coventry Inner Ring Road in order to allow a tandem marathon which would include blind and partially sighted adults and children *stokers* to take place?" The ring road which measures 2.2 miles per circuit could provide an ideal safe route whilst at the same time enabling the participants to experience the exhilaration of speeding down the flyovers and into the tunnel underpasses, climb the various gradients and enjoy the varied scenery. The full marathon would consist of 12 laps but the beauty of this course was that the participants could decide themselves how many laps they did, dependent upon fitness and energy.

We felt that the event should be a fun one, so why not invite participants to ride in fancy dress with the opportunity of involving the family; bearing the latter in mind resulted in the team component being introduced which meant that a solo rider could accompany each tandem. Tandem and solo would ride together as a Team.

We had to decide where the start and finish would be situated. The Provost made the brilliant suggestion, "Why not use the Coventry Cathedral ruins, it would make a magnificent setting. Being enclosed and away from the main traffic areas, it would provide a safe collecting and administration area for participants, families and spectators alike." Bearing in mind the difficulties caused by our visual impairment, it sounded good. Yes, we could raise funds by riders being sponsored and at the same time raise public awareness. It would introduce visually impaired adults and children to the possibilities of cycling; for children, in particular, it would be a great experience of riding on a public road in a safe environment but still with the atmosphere, but with the roar of all the traffic now using the other side of the ring road; it all had its attractions.

The Provost reminded us of Coventry's internationally acclaimed theme *Spirit of Reconciliation* and suggested it might be possible to pair riders from opposing factions riding on a tandem as a positive sign of this. It all sounded good but what about the organisation of such an event, who would support us? Could we really get the ring road closed? What would it entail? It had never been done before; the thought was so overwhelming that we put it on the back burner.

Not so the Provost, a couple of months later he telephoned to say. "Remember that idea of using the ring road for a tandem marathon, well it's on. We need a meeting in order to invite interested parties, form a committee and sort out the difficulties and get it organised; please could you arrange it?"

Well I did and the first meeting involving all those interested took place in the Provost's study. They included the Police, Fire and Ambulance services together with representatives from the local bus services, WMPTE, Coventry Cycling Club and Coventry City Council Leisure Services. A steering committee was formed.

When I looked around the group and discussions began, I quickly realised just how involved the work of staging this marathon would be. I found myself asking the question, "What am I doing here?" I need not have worried: the enthusiasm of everyone for the project and willingness to work together in order to make it happen was inspiring.

The police took responsibility to ensure safety by closing off roads and diverting all traffic onto the clockwise section of the ring road; the fire and ambulance services would reroute, except in an emergency when they would reserve the right to halt the marathon and use our carriageway; the bus companies agreed to reroute their services and the city council agreed to prepare and issue the temporary street closure notices required. We were also extremely fortunate in having, as a member of the steering committee, David Toomes of the Coventry Cycle Club, whose vast practical experience in organising cycle events around the country, and in particular in Coventry, was to prove so beneficial.

It all came together on Sunday 11th July 1993, the day chosen for the first Coventry Tandem Team Marathon to take place, which became a regular event. Thirty two tandems accompanied by 16 solo cyclists took part in this first ever Tandem Team Marathon held in Coventry and maybe in the U.K. Coventry's Cathedral ruins provided an unusual but magnificent setting for the Start and Finish. One family team came in fancy dress as Pirates.

The weather on the day was a mixed bag with a terrific downpour at the halfway stage ensuring everyone got a real soaking. It lasted for about 3 laps so by the time the finish was reached some people were beginning to dry out. I can tell you the refreshments and drink provided were very welcome. Participants travelled from as far away as Torquay, London and Boston in Lincolnshire. Coventry, I believe, provided the highest age when both *pilot* and *stoker's* ages added together came to 143 years. Two blind lady *stokers*, 71 and 68 years, the latter not having ridden on a tandem for 35 years, completed the 12 laps; they had got soaked but were triumphant and suffered no after effects other, I am pleased to report, than the usual stiffness.

Another of our Coventry lady *stokers*, until 2 months previously had never ridden on a cycle of any description before and like all the others completed the 12 laps, thoroughly enjoying every minute of it so much in fact that she put her name down for the following year.

For most of the local blind or partially sighted *stokers* this was the culmination of a long cherished ambition to ride a tandem and to experience the wind and rain on your face. They could hear the sounds around them, especially the cheering and clapping of the supporters and spectators lining the circuit and the words of encouragement from other team members as they encouraged you to make even greater efforts as they passed you or vice-versa. It was an opportunity for healthy exercise and fresh air working as a team member, enjoying being a part of the real world, the sighted world.

Starter for the event was Gary Liversedge, Business Sales Manager for the local area of the T.S.B. and leading off were the originators of the event, the Provost and myself. Our tandem, a Butler racing machine which used to belong to the famous Reg Harris, was kindly loaned for the event by Alan and Sue Glew of Kenilworth Wheelers.

The marathon attracted coverage from central TV News and the local radio station BBC-CWR did us proud. Two of their presenters, Ridanne Sheridan and Duncan Stanworth, actually participated, riding as solo outriders. We were also very pleased to welcome another celebrity riding with us from Birmingham's Queen Alexandra College. This was Tommy Godwin who won two bronze medals in the 1948 Olympics.

The experiences enjoyed by all the participants, particularly the blind and partially sighted, motivated them to explore the possibilities of riding all the year round and participate in other events such as the Spalding Tulip Marathon. So it was in September 1993 that a group of us, sighted and blind and partially sighted participants, got together in the day centre at Coventry Society for the Blind and formed Coventry VISTA (Visually Impaired and Sighted Tandem Association).

A committee comprising 4 blind and partially sighted people, together with four able bodied sighted cyclists, was established their objective being to develop and promote a facility which would encourage healthy exercise. At the same time it would provide the ability to get out and enjoy the countryside and fresh air, participate in sporting events, establish and enjoy friendship with both blind and partially sighted and able bodied sighted people with like interests.

In addition social activities designed to include the families of the members was to be promoted and developed especially during the winter months when cycling is restricted. The hard work, commitment and dedication of the members since those early days has seen the group develop into a healthy vibrant organisation equipped with twelve modern light-weight tandems, its own purpose designed and built tandem storage and maintenance building, all the necessary safety equipment including reflective clothing and helmets.

Drying off the dogs after a muddy walk on a Vista weekend

Members of both genders with a broad range of ages, some of whom have both visual and hearing difficulties enjoy a full diary of events which can be found on the Coventry VISTA web site – www.coventry-vista.org.

The group has also achieved registered charity status, their charity number is 1133237.

CHAPTER 12

WHAT! A PANTOMIME.

If you thought that live theatre was only for the able-bodied then read on. In 1991 I was approached by Matt Watts, audience development officer at the Belgrade Theatre Coventry,

With Gary at a pre-show picnic

to see if I was interested in live theatre and if so, would I consider joining Coventry Belgrade Theatre's access group. This group comprises people with various disabilities working with able-bodied people, all of whom are volunteers. In order to balance the group a visually impaired person was needed, hence my invite.

The group's role was that of access consultants to the theatre, not just in terms of access to the building and its services, but also the productions.

chapter twelve

It's the live theatre productions which form the subject of this part of my story and in particular the Belgrade Theatre's development of Pantomime Pre-Show Picnics.

Are you thinking like I used to? Live theatre, sadly that's not for the visually impaired, so what's the point of going? I wouldn't be able to see the production and even if a friend came with me and described what was going on-stage I would feel embarrassed by the whispering in my ear whilst the people around us were *shushing*. No, it just wasn't worth the hassle. That's a sad reflection and a view which I know from my experience of talking to visually impaired people, especially the parents of visually impaired children, many shared.

How to address this problem and open up live theatre to all, in particular those who are visually impaired, became a challenge for the Belgrade's Access Group and so we set about addressing the various difficulties.

Our first step was to work with the production director and cast of the theatre's community company which included several members with various disabilities. This was in 1992 and the production was a play-cum-musical called *Diamonds in the Dust*. Its plot centred around the activities and lives of a group of New Age travellers, who were roaming the English countryside in pursuit of musical raves. I, being the only visually impaired member of the group at that time, became the sounding board for ideas and tester for the practical experiences. I well remember being guided up onto the stage before the show commenced in order to get a feel for the space. I walked its length and width and I remember being impressed by the cavernous space indicated by the echoing sound and the feeling of emptiness and coldness. I felt the set which was very simple but evidently very effective visually. My fingers were gently guided over plastic piping (rain water pipes) which had been coated with an adhesive onto which sand had been thrown; they represented the poles of a Bedouin tent-like structure and I felt the silk-like material and shape of the tent itself.

Then it was time to meet the cast, to hear them describe their various individual roles in the production and get an idea of how they were dressed.

My first shock came when I met Tony who was quite a big lad; he played the leading role. Why shock? Well when I, at his suggestion, felt his hair it was in dreadlocks which felt very strange to me, not being accustomed to walking around feeling dreadlocks. He then took my hand and guided my fingers over his jacket which was leather and studded, like those I remember Hell's Angels used to wear. He was also wearing a heavily studded belt and had thick rings on his fingers, which all added up to giving the impression of him being an unsavoury character, which of course he was. In contrast the leading lady was dressed in a long, loose fitting, flowing dress and the material had a satin feel to it. The most striking feature about her was her jewellery; she had long, very tactile ear rings and large ankle bands, which when she moved about jingled and jangled which made it very easy to know where she was on stage.

This first exercise was very tentative, but it did prove to us that by concentrating on the use of the senses other than sight we could make live theatre more meaningful. It was a learning curve for all of us and one thing that wasn't lacking was ideas and enthusiasm.

chapter twelve

It was not enthusiasm, however, that I found when I talked to groups of visually impaired people in those early days; they all seemed resigned to staying home and listening to radio or talking books. Now, if it was a pantomime they said, we would consider coming to that because we all remember the fairy stories and there's lots of fun and laughter so maybe we would try that. In spite of this apparent lack of interest, I was able to encourage a small group of visually impaired people, five students on training class at Guide Dogs at Leamington, to try out our ideas. They were rather sceptical, but it made a welcome break in the training schedule. After their exploration of the stage set and costumes they became quite excited and keen, looking forward very much to experiencing the production itself. We knew then that we were on the right track.

Remembering what those visually impaired groups had said to me about preferring to come to a pantomime, we decided to take them at their word and set about concentrating our future development work around the pantomime. Our first action was to make contact with David Mumford, who used to be my mobility officer; it was he who gave me the confidence to use a long cane and thus regain my independence. He was now Assistant Director of the Royal Leicester and Rutland Society for the Blind, but more to the point was Chairman of the National Organisation of Drama for the Visually Impaired.

The other contact at that time was Iain Lauchlan, playing the dame as well as being script writer, producer and director of the Belgrade pantomimes. Matt Watts was the driving force behind this development, so one afternoon in late summer a group of us, David, Iain, Jane Hytch, Artistic Director and board member and myself sat down in the theatre café to discuss how we were going to approach this challenge, what were the difficulties and how could they be solved.

Every one was very enthusiastic, especially Iain who was eager to produce a pantomime that was accessible and enjoyed by all. He had brought to the meeting a copy of the draft script for *Jack and the Beanstalk*, which was to be the forthcoming pantomime, for us to pass comment on and he was prepared to incorporate any practical suggestions which we came up with.

It was at this meeting that the now famous *Scratch and Sniff* cards idea was born; it came as a result of us trying to find a way of identifying, for the visually impaired person, the scene that was on stage at any particular time during the performance. After a good deal of deliberation we decided smell was the most effective method, but wafting the smell out into the auditorium through the air conditioning system was not practical. But what about those perfume cards that ladies' magazines sometimes carry when a new perfume is being introduced to the market? Maybe we could develop that idea and give all members of the audience a card with a different smell at each corner. On a given signal from the dame on stage during the performance one of these

Eric Selby in the giant's kitchen

corners could be scratched and the exposed smell sniffed and thus a clue given as to what scene was on stage. For example Gorgonzola Cheese for the giant's smelly socks drying in his kitchen, which had everyone cringing in their seats, whereas sweet rose smells indicated a country garden. This idea, whilst being introduced to assist the visually impaired, was enjoyed by everyone and didn't separate them out by making them special.

Drawing on the experiences gained from *Diamonds in the Dust* we knew that we had to approach the design and production of both scenery and costumes from a different perspective. We needed to make them tactile and to reduce the number of cloth back-drops which had the scenes painted on them to give a 3-D effect. These, whilst being excellent visually, were not a bit of use if you couldn't see them.

The costume designs needed to incorporate materials of different textures in order to provide tactile clues of both their design and of the character wearing them. For those who are partially sighted the colours used on both the scenery painting and costume material needed to be bold, bright and clean. In this respect the questions raised were: "What colours? And how are they interpreted by visually impaired people?" This latter question led to a good deal of discussion, the result of which was to classify all the good characters in warm colours (nice to touch) such as reds, pinks, greens and yellows and the baddies in cold colours such as black, greys and blues. In deciding to adopt this approach, experience is proving that we were also earning an unanticipated bonus; our pantomime audiences are now commenting on how clean, bright and attractive the settings are, so everyone is benefiting.

How could we provide an idea of the scale of things for people who cannot see? For example how large is the giant in *Jack and the Beanstalk* when compared with the size of Mum or Dad? We solved that one by having separate *feelies* and had a spare giant's boot made that the children could examine and feel comparing it to the size of their own shoes. A spare set of giant's cutlery was also made and I well remember one little 4 year old girl's reaction when we placed the knife and fork on each side of her. When she touched them and realised they came up to the top of her shoulders she exclaimed, "What a big mouth he must have!"

We even had a beanstalk that grew and grew and grew right off stage around the auditorium and out into the foyer. The local school children grew it, or rather made the leaves and stalk in *papier maché* to the theatre pattern designs, each school coming into the theatre to add on their section. We encouraged them to

Feeling the size of the giant's underpants

put messages on the leaves both in Braille and large print. By involving schools in this way we were both raising awareness of our project and gaining positive PR for the theatre. In a later pantomime, *Beauty and the Beast,* we invited the school children to make *papier maché* masks of how they thought the beast's face would look; these were very tactile and were placed in the foyer, decorating the walls, but within easy reach of exploring fingers.

So far we had addressed the senses of touch and smell but what about hearing? Remembering how the earrings and ankle bands jingled and jangled when the leading lady in *Diamonds in the Dust* moved around on stage thus enabling me to pinpoint where she was, was proof that audible components incorporated into the costume design would be helpful. Associating a particular bar of music with a specific character would also assist in the recognition of that character when it appeared on stage; for instance when the fairy appears she was accompanied by a tinkling of bells and in contrast, when the dame appears there is a trumpet fanfare and so on, each character having their own signature tune. Music: every pantomime has its own special panto song in which everyone joins, the song sheet usually being suspended high up over the stage where everyone can read the words, with the exception of course of the visually impaired. In order that the visually impaired could join in the singing along with their sighted peers and therefore feel no different, we produced the song sheets in Braille, large print and on audio cassette issuing them when the seats were booked; the children and the not-so-young children then had the opportunity of learning the simple tune and words before they came to the show.

Realising now the importance of access to information we went on to produce the pantomime programme in accessible formats: Braille, large print and on audio cassette but we didn't however include the adverts. Subsequently we produced a panto introduction sheet which was given out at the box office and mailed to the visually impaired groups, schools and talking newspapers in the Midlands area in order to promote our work within the visually impaired communities. The sheet comprised an introduction to live theatre from a blind person's perspective, a brief explanation of the work of the access group, a brief description of the panto story line with the Pre-show Picnic booking details including information relating to performance dates, times and prices, in the same accessible formats.

It did not stop there either: when a visually impaired person booked their seat at the theatre's box office they were shown a tactile seating plan from which they are able to select the seat of their choice; tactile plans of the foyer, restaurant and service areas were also under development.

Why did we call our pre-show experiences *Picnics*? Well children generally love picnics which of course include food and a drink, so what better to complete our programme, which lasted about an hour and a half, than a picnic. Local companies sponsored the light refreshments which generally consisted of a doughnut, or cheese and biscuits for those suffering from diabetes, together with an orange drink or coffee.

The last component to complete our package which brought theatre alive for visually impaired people like me, was the installation of an audio description system. I first became aware of the difference that a description of what is happening on stage when it is actually occurring, makes to the total enjoyment and perception of the performance, by accident. It happened on the VIP invitation night of the *Beauty and the Beast* pantomime. I had already sat through a couple of the performances and thoroughly enjoyed them all, but this time Isobel, a member of the theatre staff, was sitting next to me. When something happened on stage to cause me to ask her what it was, she then proceeded to give me a running commentary of what was happening, and do you know, the pantomime suddenly took on a new exciting dimension; it had become a more meaningful and even more enjoyable pantomime, different from my initial perception.

I was able to understand why people suddenly burst out laughing for no apparent reason. I was amazed to hear that one scene had a castle complete with its ramparts on which a sword duel was fought; the baddie was defeated and fell onto the stage below. It was good to be warned when a bang was coming in order that I didn't jump out of my skin and to have

Exploring the Dame's amazing costume

the characters' facial expressions described especially when the *slapstick* part was taking place. My excited conversation with Isobel afterwards, during our VIP reception, had one or two of the VIPs eavesdropping and seemingly becoming quite excited too, so much so that offers of possible assistance in funding an audio description system were forthcoming.

As the Pre-show Picnics got under way, we found that everyone involved in the theatre started to take an interest and lend their support. The pantomime cast, obviously a little hesitant at first, entered wholeheartedly into the spirit of things, becoming very quickly aware of the excitement and enjoyment everyone was deriving from their experiences. In order to assist the actors to feel more comfortable and confident in their new and unusual roles, we gave them some basic training in the techniques we were using to enable visually impaired people to access live theatre by using their other senses of touch, hearing and smell.

We talked about the wide variations in the amount of sight loss in different eye conditions, how to approach a visually impaired person, how to take their hand and guide it over their costumes, as well as simple guiding techniques. A similar training course was implemented for the front of house staff, but with more emphasis on the guiding techniques and general services approach. The overall objective was to provide a warm, caring, friendly and relaxed atmosphere for everyone.

In all our pantomimes the dame's costumes are very outrageous and very, very tactile; Iain Laughlin sees to that. Examples of this have been Widow Twankey's outfit which consisted of a upside down plastic washing up bowl hat with a sink plunger sticking out of the top, tooth brush ear rings, a necklace made from sink plugs, wide hooped dress in gingham pattern with a plastic apron onto which had been bonded big plastic bubbles like those you find in bubble wrap. Doc. Martin's boots and football socks finished off the very tactile and colourful outfit.

I also remember a milkmaid's hat in *Jack and the Beanstalk* created like a Dutch girl's national headdress with side pieces which curled up and away from the ears complete with a long bright yellow pigtail; another hat was created as a football pitch complete with players. The children had lots of fun exploring these.

In contrast the baddies in *Dick Whittington* were rats from the sewers of London and were named King Rat and his two henchmen, Scratch and Sniff. They wore very tactile costumes designed to be of a much more sinister nature. King Rat wore a black peaked hat with a visor that came almost flat on his nose with a jewelled name badge on the front and big brown rat ears attached. His jacket and trousers were black leather, the trousers were laced up on the outside of each leg. A sign of his prowess as King were the rats' tails which he wore suspended from the sleeves, waist and the back of his jacket indicating his conquests; the jacket had metal studs like a biker's outfit. Of course the rats would not have been complete without false round noses with whiskers projecting from each side, a single large tooth which fitted over the actor's own teeth and a pair of wire half spectacles; their tails were fitted into the seats of their trousers. King Rat was much larger than Scratch and Sniff and he also wore a sequined purple vest under his jacket and his tail was longer and thicker than the others.

Just imagine the fun the children had exploring these costumes. I would have dearly loved to have been able to see the expressions on their faces. In contrast I will always remember the principal boy taking my hand and placing it on her fishnet-clad long shapely legs for me to feel the surprisingly quite thick but very strong net; that sent a flutter I can tell you and I didn't get my face slapped.

The princess in our pantos was always stunningly beautiful of course! A sense of her being very special was conveyed by her voice, hair and dress, which was usually quite simple, with uncomplicated panelling, a lace-up bodice, a halter neck and three quarter length sleeves and full length skirt. The skirt material had a fine delicate tactile pattern, the bodice material usually has a velvet feel to it whilst the blouse was of a contrasting material, silk or cotton with fine lace trim. The good fairy was easy to recognise with a star headdress and dress with low cut neckline tight fitting bodice and short *tutu* skirt that stuck out all round. She also wore ballerina tights and ballet shoes, not forgetting the butterfly-like wings which no fairy could be without. The fairy's long-handled magic wand with its very tactile star completed the outfit.

In the later pantomimes we found that the costume colours are much enhanced by panelling them; that is using the stained glass window system of containing the coloured glass profiles with leading separating the colours from each other. This was done by using black piping, which we were advised was very effective.

In parallel with this work, provision was being made for similar access for people who are hearing impaired. People who are qualified sign interpreters were used to sign the performance to the hearing impaired audiences. By incorporating them into the panto cast their signing was not obvious to the general audience. Two sign interpreters were used, one playing the role of a *baddie* and one playing the part of a *goodie*; the hearing impaired members of the audience were advised which was which. In the same way as Braille, large print and audio were being used to provide information about the pantomime for those who are visually impaired, videos which used sign interpreters to convey the spoken and written word were being developed and produced for those people with a hearing impairment. The theatre staff received training in disability awareness and how to meet the needs of people with disabilities when they visit the theatre.

I was normally involved in these training sessions in which I discussed theatre from a visually impaired person's perspective. I used shades (spectacles which assimilate various eye conditions) to explain how the amount of vision or light perception can vary from one visually impaired person to another and explained the difference in concept between a generically visually impaired person to one who has enjoyed sight. I found it helped to generate confidence if the cast can practise guiding on me in a relaxed atmosphere, taking my hands and guiding my fingers over their costumes describing, as they do so, the various aspects of their design. It was a very rewarding experience to feel the positive attitude and after that initial embarrassment the confidence and motivation which this work is generating within all those involved.

Since the Belgrade led the way, touch tours of sets and costumes have now become regular events in theatres as well as audio described and signed performances.

CHAPTER 13

EXPERIENCES IN COOMBE ABBEY COUNTRY PARK
A sensual exploration and a dawn chorus

What does a country park mean to you? Large areas of rolling parkland with a big house sitting in the middle of it? Lots of trees, oak, ash, cedars pines or even a redwood? Water, lakes, rivers and streams? Birds: herons standing silent and serene on one leg, like statues in the water, kingfishers, a flash of blue and

Country Matters in the Telegraph: Duff Hart-Davis wrote about how I enjoy walks in the ocuntryside

a splash, wild ducks and geese? Animals: rabbits, deer maybe foxes and badgers? Open spaces: lovely gardens, statues, lots of colour and an idyllic settings ideal for relaxation?

But what if you are blind or partially sighted? Not for you this grand vista on which you feast your eyes, but it can still be that place of beauty, intrigue and peace. It is important however to remember that a country park to a blind or partially sighted person is not the same as it is to a sighted one. To a sighted person everything is visual, you open your eyes and there it is instantly available. For those who are blind, accessing this instant picture is not possible because we have to build our picture block by block using our other senses.

I am encouraged by the greater awareness and understanding of the needs of people with disabilities now being shown by the management of a growing number of our country parks and historic buildings, who are making positive commitments in order to provide access to their parks and buildings for all. This new approach presents many exciting and challenging opportunities with the application of proven ideas and systems. These include, the major component in any successful project, listening seriously to the needs, experiences and ideas of the potential users and learning from them. The provision of access for all, in addition to bringing the pleasures of the countryside and our nation's historic buildings within the reach of those people with disabilities, also, in commercial terms, increases the potential customer base.

The following are just a few examples of ideas currently being used which are enabling visually impaired people to access the countryside:

- Footpaths which have varying tactile surfaces such as gravel, brick, metal, grass, sand and wood planks, all serve as aids to guide and locate.
- Guiding tap rails which made up of wooden boards placed on edge. These are located along the sides of the path projecting approx 6 inches above its surface and they also serve to retain the path material, thus preventing the path crumbling away at its edges.
- Concrete edging kerbstones or tiles, bricks or even lawn edging will serve the same purpose. This projecting surface serves as a guide tap rail for those people using a mobility cane or as a cane trail board for those being guided by a Guide Dog.
- Simple tactile models and plans illustrating the park layout together with the different places of interest, including tactile diagrams and pictures of animals and

Recording the sounds of the countryside

insects. These to be located on site in the areas where they live, plus being available in a reduced size for people to purchase and take away to study or keep as a souvenir of their visit.

- Sighted information covering the park and its buildings should be made available in a format readily accessible to visually impaired people, such as Braille, large print and audio.

Exploring the trunk of a large tree

The introduction of at least some if not all of these ideas will encourage visually impaired people to come and explore and enjoy the park for themselves, either independently, or in small groups.

Combining this with guiding and an informative audio which is specially recorded in the actual positions referred to on the walk, not only gives you instructions to guide you along the route but also describes the scenery at that particular point. Additional relevant information can be included, such as creatures that may be living in that locality with the sounds they make, just in case you should not hear them during your visit.

Now, I would like to invite you to join me on one of my walks, share in my experiences which will hopefully help you to understand my perception of this park. Today I've chosen Coombe Abbey Park which is situated on the outskirts of Coventry.

I should first warn you, in order that you don't get embarrassed, about my tree hugging activities. This involves putting my arms around a tree and feeling its size. I also feel the bark, whether it is hard or soft, at the same time noting its texture. Is it smooth or fibrous? Are there cracks in it where small insects and animals can hide and take shelter? Are there holes where birds can nest? How big is the base, are the roots exposed and what about the leaves, what size and shape are they? Do they smell? I know the children who visit Coombe love a particular coniferous tree because its leaves smell like *Opal Fruit* sweets (now called *Starburst*); in fact they called it the *Opal Fruit Tree*.

I walk on past the lake where I can hear the mallards making their low quacking noises and splashing about in the water. The sound is different! I walk a little further and I hear water babbling over stones; it's a small stream and as I walk on the sound changes. It's louder now, no longer gentle and peaceful but rushing and roaring as it passes over a weir and then, what was that? I hear a Reed Warbler. I was the first to spot it as those who were sighted had not seen it, so that pleased me.

The footpath texture changes, I hear the crunch of gravel under my feet, different to the soft and slightly damp soil section of path that I have just left. Now we reach the lake and my friend describes the scene. He tells me about the herons, how many pairs there are, how they fish, describes the kingfisher and now I can hear the Canada geese over on the far side of the lake; I think to myself wouldn't it be nice if I could have an audio recording of all these sounds that I could take home with me to keep as a souvenir of my visit.

We turn to make our way back and soon I feel a different surface under foot; it's wooden planks, made into a kind of bridge and we are now in an area called the wet area. I can smell the dampness around me and the foliage feels lush and thick. I can smell different scents wafting on the breeze from the various plants around me.

What's that underfoot? It's a mole hill! My friend removes the spoil which forms the hill exposing the mole's tunnel and invites me to put my finger into the hole. At first I decline, wondering where the mole might be, but eventually I do and am surprised to find the hole is only just a little larger than my finger and the tunnel walls are very smooth. I realise that is the first time that I have done that and I must have seen and fallen over hundreds of mole hills when I was sighted.

Continuing on my way I feel with my fingers the different grasses and reeds. I learn about the duck decoy, its purpose and how it was built. The path around this section has recently been relaid and has a wooden tap rail along its complete route, so I get some practice in with my mobility cane; as I walk I find a series of very tactile ceramic tiles, each one measuring approximately 12 inches square and depicting pictures of things which live or can be seen in that particular locality. The tiles have been painted in colours which are easily identified by people with partial sight. They will withstand the effects of weathering and are held securely in metal stands in sets of four at a height which is accessible to people in wheelchairs.

The tiles are very tactile; I can feel a large frog on one tile, tadpoles on another and what's this? It must be a heron standing on one leg. And now I can hear the herons calling to each other up in the nearby trees. This brings me to the next set of tiles which depict the four seasons, showing trees over the year. A point of interest here: these tiles where designed and produced for this walk in Coombe Abbey Country Park by a group of local visually impaired people.

Now we have reached the ornamental garden. I reach out to feel the griffons which stand on either side of the steps. My fingers travel over their rough and weather-beaten surfaces, feeling the shape of the eyes and bodies. How large they are! I walk on feeling more statues and what is this in the wall? It's a section of fan vaulting removed from the abbey many years ago, very fine stonework, very delicate. I sit and rest on a garden seat and relax and

Feeling the stone carving at Coombe Abbey Country Park

as I do so I can smell the different fragrances being given off by the many flowers and herbs around me and I try to list all those that I recognise. I relax and enjoy the feeling of space. I listen to the wind rustling the leaves and think to myself how different this would be in the winter, so I must come again.

Indeed I have visited again, many times, encouraged by the management staff of the park and my friends from the Dog Rose Trust, who have not only taken a keen interest, but have been actively involved in developing and promoting the ways and means of opening up the countryside to people with disabilities. I have appreciated their invitation to work with them on these projects which in addition to giving me so much pleasure and relaxation has, at the same time, developed my own confidence and knowledge, showing me ways of thinking positively which hopefully I can pass on to others. Each time I visit I discover a different aspect or enjoy a new experience.

I well remember one such occasion: it was during a visit, the purpose of which was to assemble ideas for a workshop which I had been asked to lead. This in turn was part of a conference entitled *In Through the Outdoors at Coombe.* It was designed to show how the countryside can be made more accessible for people with disabilities. Emma, the park's education ranger, told me about a game which she had devised for the school children that regularly visited the park; the idea was to invite the children to produce a *Smelly Cocktail* and then to give their cocktail a descriptive name which best described the overall smell that they had produced. They were each given a plastic cup and a small spatula with which to stir their leaf cocktail. The children were then instructed to explore an area in the park looking for leaves which were smelly. They then decided which of these smelly leaves they would use in their cocktail, picked the respective leaf or leaves, put them into the vending cup, giving them a stir with the spatula and depending upon the resulting smell, nice or otherwise, chose a name for the concoction.

 Another game was to give the children small cards onto which had been glued different manmade materials, such as *Fuzzy Felt* on one and a piece of coarse sand paper on another. Armed with these the children were then asked to explore an area in the park, with the objective of finding surfaces which, in their opinion, best resembled the feel of the sample materials on their cards. In Coombe Park the *Fuzzy Felt* very closely resembled the feel of the bark to be found on the Redwood trees and the sand paper, the texture found on stone walling. By using these techniques the children were being encouraged to use their other senses, and not relying on their eyes alone. This created an awareness of the tactility and smells of plants, trees, shrubs and living things by encouraging them to use their other senses; in other words discovering the countryside as we visually impaired do.

A DAWN CHORUS

Another unforgettable experience was a walk in the park at 5 am in order to experience the Dawn Chorus. I joined a group of visually impaired folk, all members of our local Coventry VISTA tandem group, together with our sighted friends who kindly acted as our guides. A 30 strong group, organised by Joe Taylor the head ranger at Coombe Abbey Country Park, met up one Saturday in early May.

The dawn chorus had always been one of those things I had wanted to experience when I was sighted, but had always put off for one reason or another. The lure of my cosy warm bed and the darkness all around me at such an unearthly time, I feel sure had something to do with it. This day however was different. Anne called for me in the car at 4.30 a.m. and in the car with her were her children: Scott, Yvonne and Gregory all very excited by the thought of this big adventure that was about to unfold. Tony, Anne's husband, had taken their other car and was collecting Jim, Jeanette and Jason, our other blind friends, the plan being to all meet up at the Visitor Centre at Coombe at around 4.50 a.m. The weather was fine, a little on the chilly side and the children told me that it was very dark. We made as little noise as was possible so as not to disturb the neighbours and there was a brief period of excitement for the children when, on an unlighted section of dual carriageway just before the park, Anne's headlights picked up a dog fox sitting in the middle of the road; he just got up and ambled to the side on our approach.

Although it was still dark the birds were already singing, a fact that I had noticed when I had got up at 4 a.m. Later Joe was to confirm that some birds had indeed been up and singing from around 2.30, which then had me wondering if we had been enticed out of our beds on false pretences. The answer to that question was an emphatic no. The exhilarating experience provided by listening to all that beautiful bird song, the special atmosphere which that time in the morning creates with its chill factor, the smell and feel of the early morning mist, its stillness and the different fragrances given off by the carpets of wild bluebells. All this was interspersed with a variety of earthy country smells which wafted about us as we walked and combined to make this a walk to remember.

The commentaries and description given by Joe and our sighted friends all contributed in making the experience meaningful and of course the bacon and egg mixed grill breakfast which had been specially prepared for us afterwards in the park's Herons Table Restaurant was a very enjoyable and satisfying finale.

I found myself so engrossed in the anticipation and savouring of the sounds and smells that abounded all around us creating that special atmosphere that I can honestly say that the fact that I was blind and couldn't see what must have been a most visually beautiful dawn, didn't cross my mind. I was using those other senses of mine to the full. I also have what will now be a treasured record of our visit; it's a stereo recording which I made during our walk and it has captured the atmosphere together with the various bird songs, each being identified by Joe. Recordings like this illustrate instances when for the visually impaired person the recording machine replaces the camera to good effect; after all you could not possibly hope to record the atmosphere one experienced in a photograph, but which a recording can. This is then available to be relived and shared with friends in comfort and relaxation at home, like sighted people share their photographs.

Let me now share a little of that walk with you and maybe you will understand in some small way the compensations that can be achieved for that which for I am missing. You join us at 5.05 a.m; Joe Taylor, the head ranger, has assembled us all at the end of the visitors' centre for a briefing prior to setting off. According to Ann, who was to guide me, there are about 30 people in a group with two families with young children and a mixture of young and elderly couples, a few individuals, some of which appear to be serious bird watching enthusiasts.Dorcas, my guide dog, is at home and I suspect still snoring her head off. I didn't bring her as I felt concerned that she might disturb the birds.

Joe tells us that due to an exceptional set of circumstances this year (1995); anyone who had been in the countryside would have realised that we have had a lot of north easterly winds which has had the effect of keeping many of the birds on the continent. These winds had now blown themselves out and as a consequence the birds were now pouring in, as if there were no tomorrow. Joe says that it's the first year that he can remember that swallows have been feeding virtually all night, as they had been last night, when they were up and around, singing and participating in a little courtship on the telegraph wires.

The black birds and thrushes were up at around 3.30, singing their sentinel song as they sat on the top of the posts and shrubs marking out their boundaries; these I could hear very clearly as they seemed to be all around us. We started to move off, heading in the direction of the lakes and as we did so Joe pointed to one of the high rise residents, a heron, who was just leaving his night's resting place, a chimney, situated on the roof of the recently restored Abbey, now converted into an upmarket Hotel. The herons also nest in the tops of the trees in the park so this area is naturally called the Heronry.

As we walk Anne describes the scene to me. Particularly striking and beautiful, on our right, is the setting of the restored abbey, its dark outline silhouetted against the lighter sky. The lights in the Abbey Hotel were all shining brightly, piercing the blackness with bright yellow rectangles of light and with the early mist swirling around its base. I began, as Ann described it, to imagine the setting to be like one of those fairy tale castle drawings often used to illustrate children's stories. The air felt pleasant and crisp and one had the feeling that the forthcoming day was going to be a warm one and indeed the weather forecast confirmed our feelings.

Our footsteps crunched on the loose gravel as we walked, the sound echoing around the building's walls and then disappearing as we walked out into the open park. We were now approaching the lake where our route would take us along the drive which cut the lake into two; the song thrushes were now getting into full song, really proclaiming that morning had broken, singing from the very tops of the trees around us. Then I heard that sharp warning note of the coot or perhaps it was a moorhen and the sound of splashing as it scurried out of our way, having heard us approaching. This told me that we must now be nearing the water, which was confirmed by the sounds of the Canada geese over on the far side of the lake; my, they are a noisy lot, with their piercing but distinctive calls.

As we walked across the lake I felt a drop in the air temperature and could hear the water making gentle lapping sounds against the sides of the drive, with the occasional low throated quacks of the mallards and a splash or two as they did a *bottoms-up* dive for food. The air seemed to be so still and clean which, with the expanse of water, seemed to accentuate the bird song which now was very loud.

The overall sound of so many birds singing their little hearts out was in itself an exhilarating experience. There were so many birds singing that we were glad that we had Joe to guide us. With his expert knowledge and fine tuned ear he was able to identify and describe the call for each bird. After leaving the lake we were walking through trees again. I felt the atmosphere and sounds change and then the *teacher, teacher, teacher* call of the members of the tit family. Joe surprised us by telling us that the Great Tit has 26 common call variations, which makes it difficult to distinguish and identify.

We were now passing the conifers and Joe was pointing out some Goldcrest nests which are tucked tightly into the branches and then I hear *chiff-chaff*, *chiff-chaff*, the song of a bird who derives its name from its sound: the Chiff Chaff. Joe describes them as little brown jobs that come over from Africa, although in this country they have developed green plumage.

Joe stops suddenly and listens, inviting us to do the same; it's the song of a Willow Warbler. Joe stops again and this time it's a Great Spotted Woodpecker. It's evidently presenting a very clear silhouette whilst it busies itself picking insects off a leaf; Joe tells us that it is very difficult to differentiate one woodpecker type from another, but they are all very noisy, presenting a lovely overall sound, a bit like an orchestra. The plumage, particularly the breast plumage of the Great Spotted Woodpecker is white, a fact which is evidently confirmed by the pictures in the reference books. Tony, Ann's husband, however was not convinced, a point which Joe readily understood. He caused some amusement when he went on to explain that when most people observe woodpeckers, they are up in the trees and look dark because they are silhouetted and if we were to spend most of our day rubbing our stomachs up and down against trees which were covered in muck and various types of lichens, as the woodpeckers do, then our stomach would be green too.

I mention to Joe that I often hear a woodpecker hammering on the trees when I am out walking in the woods near where I live. "That's a territorial sound he's making," advises Joe and he goes on to say, "If you get really tuned in to woodpecker calls you can identify different woodpeckers by listening to the drumming and counting the number of seconds pause in between. There is a difference in the length of these periods, which enables you to identify either the Great or the Lesser Spotted Woodpecker.

Suddenly I smelt a sweet heavy perfume being wafted around me and at the same time Ann gasped, "Oh isn't that beautiful, can you smell them? There is a huge expanse of bluebells growing here and they are presenting a lovely carpet of blue spreading between the trees, covering the floor for as far as I can see." At this stage in our walk, it is just beginning to become light but the sun isn't up yet. The time is now 5.45 and my stomach is telling me that all this exercise is making me hungry and reminding me of that mixed grill breakfast to come.

We walked on, with the scent of the blue bells seeming to linger around us for ever. Joe's stopped. What's that he's saying? A Willow Warbler is practising his notes, running up and down the scale. I would never have been able to identify that; it just shows how important it is to have such a knowledgeable enthusiastic expert with one on such a walk as this. Ah! now that is a sound that I do recognise; it's a cuckoo calling from deep in the woods and today is Saturday May 5th 1995, the day I heard my first cuckoo call of the year. Summer must now be really on its way and after that excitement we heard the song of the wren, a tiny little bird which I can just about remember, as it used to feature on the back of the old farthing copper coins.

Anne tweaks my arm, and explains, "The sun has just this minute appeared, it's low down on the horizon and is just peeping through the trees, it's fiery red in colour" and the way Ann is describing it, it is presenting a romantic picture like the ones I remember seeing on chocolate boxes, an impression which seems to be confirmed by Tony, who has just whispered to Ann, "If there weren't all these people around it would be quite romantic."

It's 6.10 now, the sun is changing in colour to a yellowy orange and Joe says that all the signs are for a great day ahead. The sun is now rising fast, giving the trees a completely different dimension. The early morning mist is hanging around the tops of the trees. Ann is telling me that as she looks through the woodland now, she can see the leaves appearing to take on different shapes, and there are drops of dew glistening on the leaves of the sycamores, sparkling like little diamonds caught in the suns rays. Ann confirms that the daylight is really increasing now. Joe stops us again, this time to observe the cobwebs which the spiders have been busy spinning and which are now hanging on the masses of burdock which border both sides of the path along which we are walking. He describes their silvery gossamer appearance to me, the weight of the dew causing some of the bigger ones to sag in the middle. He tells me that you can see the little spiders lying in wait for their prey in the middle of the web, which shouldn't be long seeing how cleverly they have been positioned in order to catch the insects flying along the path. I put out my hand and feel for one of these webs and very gently I touch it, my fingers being guided by Ann. It feels very delicate and kind of clingy; a dew drop falls onto my finger and trickles into my hand. Immediately recollections of the cobwebs which I can remember seeing in my sighted days, after a hard frost spring to mind, and I realise how fortunate I am in having access to these picture memories which are now stored in my mind from the days when I could see, compared with Jeanette who is generically blind and as a consequence has never seen; she is also feeling a spider's web as she stands just behind me and I begin to wonder, what does the spider's web mean to her?

I began to feel a different atmosphere; it was colder and I could now hear the sounds of the rest of the human race beginning to stir, but the sound was not at all intrusive, considering we were only about 4 miles from the centre of Coventry. I was able to pick out from the gentle constant murmur of what must be general traffic noise and the sound of a far distant train rumbling along.

I had been conscious of the path rising over the last couple of hundred yards or so and now the change was explained by Ann. "We have now walked out into a large field, which is often used as a picnic area, which explains your awareness of a change in atmosphere and the different sounds coming from suburbia." "Watch out! Be careful." shouts Yvonne, Ann's daughter, who has been walking just in front of us. "There's an awful lot of rabbit holes and mole hills around here, so be careful where you are putting your feet as you could easily trip over." Ann then watches me closely, guiding me to ensure that doesn't happen and I remember that this must be the place where, on a previous walk, I had put my finger down inside one of these mole hills feeling the mole's run and tell her about it. "I can see a large area of feathers and fluff just over there, to our left; it looks as if the foxes dined well last night," Ann observes "And there are a lot of rabbit droppings scattered around here," indicating the rabbit population didn't seem to be at too great a risk from these predators.

Upon leaving the open field the path descended, returning us via a winding route through the trees back to the lake. The bird song was now much lower in volume, the birds concentrating upon getting food. We can hear a nuthatch singing in the bushes on our right; he must have been a late starter. This return leg of our walk is planned to take in a specially constructed bird hide which allows access for wheelchairs and observation windows at low level as well as the normal heights, a bonus for the children; the sound of our footsteps change to a hollow echo which tells me that we must be approaching it. Ann confirms that we have arrived and describes it as being a long, low wooden cabin projecting from its short side out into the lake with. Open slots in its sides enable people to view the birds with their binoculars or take photographs with their cameras. I feel out of place here, a bit useless, so I stay in the entrance to the hide with my back against a wall whilst the other sighted folk go and observe.

I listen to Joe describing the scene and answering questions about the herons and cormorants which consume large quantities of fish from the lake daily and also goldfish from the garden pools of more than a few local Coventry residents. I find Joe very informative and interesting and become absorbed in creating my own mental picture following his descriptions.

Here is where an audio guide and audio information would be useful. I listen to the water fowl: I can hear the coots clucking, the herons calling to their mates high up in the trees and those Canada geese are still creating a racket, at times nearly blocking out all the bird song. But wait a minute! There is that Reed Warbler practising his scales again and someone has just seen the blue flash of a Kingfisher. Evidently everyone has now experienced the hide so Joe again leads the way.

As we walk I can feel brief periods of warmth on the left hand side of my face and shoulders. It's the sun I can feel, giving off its warmth as it rises higher and higher in the morning sky, its rays piercing through the trees as I walk. This time we are heading back across the lake to the Visitor Centre from where we commenced our walk 2 hours ago.

It is now 7 a.m. and we are all gathered around Joe outside the Centre, where he is summing up and telling us about other guided walks that the centre rangers organise. Suddenly everyone starts laughing and I ask Ann and the children what's happening. They tell me that a family of squirrels have decided to come out and give the group the once-over; they became the centre of attraction as they practised hurdling along the ranch fencing along on our right. Scott is giving me a commentary and it sounds good fun for everyone.

Thank you Joe, that was excellent. "What did you think? Jeanette, Jim, are you there Jason?" "I didn't realise that the bird song was so loud and that there were so many different birds," replies Jeanette. "I wouldn't have missed it, it was worth getting up for," said Jason, adding, "Scott was a good guide although," with laughter in his voice, "he did try to compete with the birds." Jim agreed that he too had thoroughly enjoyed the experience. This was an experience that would not have been possible had it not been for the kind assistance of our sighted friend and Joe who made the whole experience so interesting and informative. Now to that mixed grill breakfast, to which, I am sure you will understand, we did full justice.

Chapter 14

A very special day: Queen Elizabeth the Queen Mother's 100th Birthday Celebrations and Pageant.

The following is a report of how I, a totally blind person perceived and enjoyed this very special day.

Was I not the lucky one? To receive an exciting and challenging invitation to participate in the Queen Mother's 100th birthday celebrations and attend the Queen Mother's 100th birthday pageant being held on Horse Guards Parade London on Wednesday July 19th 2000.

I was to be the guest of the Royal National Institute for the Blind (RNIB), one of the considerable number of charities with which the Queen Mother had been associated for many years.

Excited? Of course I was. I have always been thrilled by the sound of military music and when I was sighted appreciated the colourful spectacle of the massed military bands marching and playing at events such as the Edinburgh Military Tattoo and Trooping the Colour in London.

I had always nurtured a secret wish to be present on Horse Guards Parade to enjoy the colourful spectacle and atmosphere of Trooping the Colour. I therefore felt very privileged to have been given this opportunity to witness and enjoy such an historic event as the Queen Mother's 100th birthday celebrations.

The challenge was that of my total blindness. Whilst I would enjoy the music, military and orchestral, together with the singing by the combined choirs and especially the atmosphere that the occasion would generate, how would not being able to see that marvellous spectacle including the Queen Mum herself, affect me? Would it hurt too much? I decided no, it wouldn't, as the event was to be audio described and from my experience of audio description in the theatres, that would fill in for my eyes and my imagination would do the rest.

How would I receive the audio description? The infra-red systems used in the theatre would not be suitable, so a radio wave transmitting system suitable for use when describing outdoor events would have to be used.

My second challenge, how would I manage without my Guide Dog Harry? Harry normally accompanied me wherever I went, including regular journeys on the train to London. This event was obviously not suitable for a Guide Dog and it would not be fair to expose Harry to the difficulties which could arise. I needed to find a sighted guide with whom I could feel relaxed and what is more to the point would have the confidence and courage to take responsibility for my safety and be able to guide me in such a difficult environment.

The third challenge was how would I cope with travelling on the London tube trains? I had not travelled on them since becoming blind. Coping with the escalators, the crowded trains together with boarding and alighting from the trains presented some daunting thoughts.

Sue Walker was an audio describer at the Belgrade Theatre in Coventry and it was suggested that she might like to share the audio description of the pageant with Veronica Hyks. Veronica was treasurer of the Audio Description Association (ADA) of which both Sue and I were members. Veronica was an experienced audio describer working with the London theatres as well as television and films. I knew Sue, having enjoyed her describing various productions at the Belgrade and she was good. An idea flashed through my mind: "Would she agree to travel to London with me? Be my companion and guide?" We didn't know each other that well, having met only through the audio describers' meetings at the Belgrade Theatre. It was a lot to ask: all that on top of the anxiety of describing such a prestigious event and for the first time in an outdoor situation with unfamiliar equipment.

I didn't think that Sue had done any previous guiding of blind people so how would she react to my suggestion if I were brave enough to make it? I plucked up the courage and Sue agreed. I had been right: she had not had any experience guiding blind people but agreed to take a crash course a couple of days before the event.

Now for the special day itself. It was full of promise, the sun was shining and it was quite warm, no rain was forecast and the adrenalin was beginning to pump in anticipation of the event which lay ahead. The train journey was comfortable and uneventful, the time was taken up with Sue and I discussing the pageant and how she would describe it. Sue was rather concerned because the essential briefing notes for the event had not been received from the RNIB.

We managed to get to Westminster tube station, our rendezvous point after initial chaos with a bomb alert. As we walked along Sue seemed to go automatically into describing mode, telling me about the area immediately around us. I remember her description of the Ministry of Defence and the statues positioned on the embankment. I remember especially the clear description of a statue of a Fleet Air Arm pilot dressed in flying suit, flying helmet and goggles with aircraft wings nestling in the fold of his arms. Nothing was lost by Sue's keen eye: for instance the white Mercedes coupé with its hood down revealing a rather attractive lady sitting at the wheel, the car being held up in the mass of traffic.

Sue's commentary was helping me to feel quite relaxed in spite of what was going on around us. "Will we make it to Horse Guards Parade? Will we find the group? The group has our admission tickets." These thoughts kept recurring and then I heard Sue say, "There is a police cordon just in front, the area is closed off, we are not going to be allowed through." Then Sue was talking to a London policeman with a Glaswegian accent who was advising her, "Sorry, this is a security alert, you can't get through. I suggest that you return to the Embankment and sort it out from there."

On the way back we paused outside the Ministry of Defence for Sue to call the RNIB on her mobile telephone for instructions; thank goodness for mobile telephones. The RNIB were on the ball, obviously already having been alerted to the difficulties members of the group were experiencing. They advised us to return to the Embankment tube station as this was the new rendezvous point and a representative was making his way there with the tickets. When we arrived back at the tube station there were even more people milling around, so how on earth were we going to find the group? One consoling thought was that Sue should be able to pick out the white canes.

Sue saw an official fielding questions from exasperated travellers so decided to approach him to ask if he could help us. As she was talking to him a voice from behind us said, "I am Karen from the RNIB and I am your contact point." We both breathed a sigh of relief: the sun began to shine again. The group, with the exception of just a couple, all eventually managed to make it to the rendezvous point, quite an achievement in the circumstances. The tickets were distributed and then we were off walking to Horse Guards Parade.

Our route took us past the end of Downing Street, the Cenotaph, White Hall and Horse Guards. Sue was busy describing the scene as we walked: tourist coaches disgorging their passengers, the heavy presence of the police and security personnel were all described. Occasionally a member of the armed forces would walk in front of us wearing full ceremonial dress; we must be nearly there I thought as the adrenalin began to pump even faster. I remember Sue telling me as we entered Horse Guards that we were passing a group of people, including children, who were clutching gift wrapped parcels, obviously hoping to give them to the Queen Mother as she passed.

Then we were suddenly out of the crowds and the traffic noise and into the relative peace surrounding the Treasury buildings and into Horse Guards Parade itself. We passed through security checks one after the other, very reassuring in the circumstances. The checks were manned by personnel from the armed forces, all very polite and friendly and seemingly relaxed. Sue described their uniforms as we passed, the sailors with their ships being notified by the names on their hat bands and the colourful and striking uniforms of the Black Watch Regiment of Canada was certainly getting my imagination into gear.

Then we were climbing the steps in the stand and being gently ushered by a friendly voice of a soldier of the Black Watch Regiment of Canada. The seats were quite comfortable and being high up gave an excellent view for those of the group who were sighted. It was hot on the parade ground but cool where we were seated. Sue was next to me and Veronica one row behind and to our left. The audio description equipment was tested and found to be operating well with a very clear signal and no interference. I was impressed; it was better reception than we experience in the theatre. One comment however: we only had one microphone and whilst this did not distract from the description, two microphones could have added to the spontaneity. We settled in our seats as Sue and Veronica described the scene for us.

The flags which were positioned all around the parade ground were fluttering in the slight breeze and were very colourful against the green of the trees and the blue of the sky. The stand in which the Royal Philharmonic Orchestra was located together with the combined choirs was positioned on the far side of the parade ground, in front and to the left of us. The combined choirs included St Paul's and Canterbury Cathedrals, Norwich girls, St Albans, St Magnus Kirkwall, Orkney Cathedral with Queen's College Cambridge and the Royal School of Music. Of special interest were the signing choir of the Royal School for Deaf Children, Margate.

Just in front of us and slightly to the right was positioned a gazebo under which a platform had been erected on which two chairs had been placed. This was obviously going to be the focal point of the celebrations because this was where the Queen Mother would sit to enjoy the pageant arranged in her honour. The sighted people in our group would have an excellent view of her.

The air of anticipation was broken by the sound of military music. The massed bands were on the march and the music became louder as they marched from our right onto the parade ground: the pageant had begun. I pinched myself, yes, I really was there and a part of this historic occasion.

The massed bands included Her Majesty's Royal Marines, the Grenadier Guards, the Irish Guards, the Welsh Guards, the Royal Air Force, the pipes and drums of the Scots Dragoon and Irish Guards and including from the commonwealth, the Black Watch Regiment of Canada. The beat of the drums and swirl of the pipes as the bands took up their positions in front of us was stirring stuff.

Entering the parade ground and very close to us on our left and from behind us came the sound of the huge kettle drums being carried by two magnificent horses accompanied by the mounted band of the Life Guards in the Blues and Royals. Fantastic! How I wished that I could see the horses with the bandsmen in their ceremonial dress. I missed the sound however of the horses' hooves on the gravel of the parade ground, but Sue told me later that this was probably due to the sand which had been dusted onto the parade ground.

chapter fourteen

Veronica was being kept busy describing the arrival of all these bands which was quite difficult, but fortunately there happened to be two mothers who had sons in the Blues and Royals sitting behind her and advising her where necessary. The parade was drawn up and ready for inspection awaiting the arrival of Her Majesty, the Queen Mother.

Then faintly at first came the sound behind us and to the left, of people cheering: the Queen Mother was on her way. The cheering grew louder and louder, being suddenly interrupted by the buglers of the Royal Marines sounding the *Alert*. Sue advised us through our headsets that the Queen Mother had arrived, she was riding in a horse drawn open carriage accompanied by a Captain's Escort of the Household Cavalry, their helmets and breast plates glistening in the sunshine. The Prince of Wales accompanied the Queen Mother in the carriage. From where we were sitting we had a good view of both the Queen Mother and Prince Charles as they entered the parade ground on our left very close to where we were sitting. The Queen Mother then inspected the troops drawn up for inspection in her honour. Having completed the inspection she took her seat on the platform under the colourful canopy.

Whilst this was happening Sue was describing the action and the clothes which the Queen Mother was wearing. The Queen Mother managed to climb the steps unaided except for the support of her walking stick. She appeared a very diminutive figure compared to Prince Charles who was keeping very close to her side.

Everyone was seated and the pageant began. The armed services formed up and marched past led by the Royal

Navy, represented by sailors from H.M.S. Dryad and Ark Royal, to the tune *Heart of Oak*. Included in the march past were representatives from the Commonwealth: the Royal Australian Medical Corps to the tune *Here's a health unto her Majesty* and the Toronto Scottish Regiment to the tune *All the blue bonnets are over the border*.

After the march past, came the release of one hundred white doves, one for each year of the Queen Mother's life. During the release of the doves the orchestra played and the choirs sang a selection of popular songs from the last ten decades. While Sue described the release of the doves I could hear the flap of their wings as they soared up into the blue sky.

Then it was the turn of the civilian organisations to march, skip or dance past to the accompaniment of the music from the past one hundred years, including music from around the nations. We were all invited to join in the singing, which brought back many memories. It was unbelievable the number of organisations with which the Queen Mother was associated and they were all represented. It would take me far too long to describe them, but it certainly kept Sue and Veronica very busy. Audio description represented the picture that I couldn't see; the colour and design of the costumes, the facial expressions and body movement would have meant very little to me without it. Obviously some of the organisations' displays remain fresh in my memory.

I mention just a few, such as the representative of the Queen Mother's household staff who had charge of two of the Queen Mother's corgis, mother and daughter who, I am afraid to say, were not behaving themselves, much to the amusement of the audience. Much better behaved and on parade were other animals belonging to the Queen Mother such as a race horse and an Aberdeen Angus bull. The RNIB were represented by Jill Allan King with her Guide Dog sitting in a vintage motor vehicle; when she passed us she got a cheer from all of us. Another organisation for the blind represented was the Birmingham Royal Institute for the Blind and The Chicken Shed Theatre Company, which included a children's and youth theatre company. They performed, with three hundred and fifty members, a special song and dance production, *100 years, the future*, especially commissioned for the day, an example of how the performing arts belong to everyone.

Of special interest to me was the fly past of the Battle of Britain memorial flight. There was no mistaking the sound of that throaty roar of those Rolls Royce Merlin engines in the Spitfire, Hurricane and Lancaster bomber as they flew over the parade ground accompanied by a Bristol Blenheim bomber and then the Red Arrows. Still the organisations marched past, including the Chelsea Pensioners from the Royal Hospital Chelsea to the tune of *The Boys of the Old Brigade*.

The Queen Mother was obviously enjoying the afternoon, frequently shielding her eyes against the sun for a better view, smiling and commenting to Prince Charles. Present in the parade were many celebrities including Dame Vera Lynn, Dame Thora Hird, Hinge and Bracket, Patricia Hodge, Barbara Windsor and Norman Wisdom. Sue told us that at one time Dame Vera Lynn, Dame Thora Hird and Barbara Windsor were sitting in the stand just a few seats from where we were sitting. When all the company were assembled it was time to sing the special birthday song accompanied by the orchestra, the combined choirs and the massed bands, pipes and drums.

Next came a most moving moment, twelve Rolls Royce cars were driven into the arena, each one a different colour including a *Silver Ghost* model. In the Rolls Royces were sitting the proud recipients of the VC, DFC and DSO medals and they received a very warm welcome from the audience. The *Silver Ghost* Rolls Royce, in which Sir John Mills CBE was sitting, drew up in front of the Queen Mother's platform. Sir John stood up in the car and facing the Queen Mother, addressed her, conveying congratulations and best wishes for a happy birthday on behalf of the nation. Sir John, who himself is nearly blind, did not read from a script but spoke from the heart, a loving tribute.

Then it was time to bring on the birthday cake complete with 100 candles. Veronica and Sue described the cake as it was assembled in front of us. 100 children, each one dressed as an individual slice of cake, came together to create the cake as a whole. I will always remember the little lad with the Cockney accent, a bossy but endearing character shouting out to his friends, the slices of cake, marshalling them into position and then with the manoeuvre successfully completed turning towards the Queen Mother wishing her a happy birthday in his broad Cockney accent. It must have brought a smile to everyone's face. We all stood and with everyone joining in sang *Happy Birthday*. As we did so I felt something falling on my head; it was the rose petal drop. Then the largest birthday card in the world was brought into the arena during the singing. When I sat down again, the lady on my right pressed something into my hand, it was a handful of rose petals which had collected at my feet. Needless to say I kept them and will keep them along with the special programme as a souvenir of the day.

Now it was the Queen Mother's turn to address all those assembled which she did in a clear unfaltering voice, which was marvellous, considering her age. This was then followed by three cheers from all those assembled which echoed all around the parade ground, the royal salute and finally the National Anthem.

All too soon it was nearly over and the Queen Mother waved to everyone. Descending the steps from the platform unaided she entered the waiting limousine and was then driven around the arena, smiling and acknowledging everyone. People were clapping, waving and cheering her as she drove past, particularly our group. Then she was gone and it was all over. I sat and reflected on what had been a truly memorable experience, a very special day.

How Sue and Veronica had been able so skilfully to complete that picture which I couldn't see, with the aid of audio description, was amazing. This was surely yet another exciting development in the never-ending quest to enable blind and partially sighted people to share in the experiences which able bodied, sighted people take for granted, thus improving the quality of our lives.

A special thank you to both Sue and Veronica for being the artists, completing that memorable picture for us, a picture which will always stay in my mind and one which will be so proudly described to my grandchildren. I was there!

CHAPTER 15

I MEET THE QUEEN

A MEMORABLE DAY

Monday November 19th 2007 was the day that Her Majesty the Queen and His Royal Highness the Duke of Edinburgh celebrated their Diamond Wedding Anniversary in Westminster Abbey. I was privileged to receive an invitation

The Queen arrives in Parliament Square

from the Jubilee Walkway Trust to attend an event involving the Queen and the Duke of Edinburgh.

Following the service of thanksgiving in Westminster Abbey Her Majesty unveiled a new panoramic panel, commissioned by the Jubilee Walkway Trust, in Parliament Square. Following this we were invited to a champagne reception in Westminster Abbey Museum hosted by the Duke of Gloucester.

Accompanied by my guide dog Wills, I was met at Euston station by my friend Peter Howell from the Dog Rose Trust. We took a taxi to the bottom of Whitehall completing the journey to Parliament Square on foot. The weather was cold with heavy squally rain which we could hear hitting the roof of the taxi. Aware that we would be standing out in the Square for a couple of hours, during which I anticipated that we would be soaked, didn't exactly excite me.

Wills and I waiting with Peter Howell to meet the Queen

I need not have worried: within ten minutes of arriving in the Square the sun came out and stayed out for the rest of the day.

The Square which is surrounded by some of London's most important buildings is cut off by roads on all sides leaving a grass area with trees in the centre with the statues

Shaking hands with the Queen

of famous statesmen such as Winston Churchill, Abraham Lincoln and most recently Nelson Mandela. At noon precisely the police closed all the roads around the square to all traffic. To get to the panel we had to pass through a security gate manned by the police, with armed policemen observing. Here we showed our passports and invitations which were then checked against the invited list.

At last we made it to the panel which is approximately 40cm high and 1.3 metres long giving easy access for wheel chair users. The panel, which has been made in etched zinc, has been designed to be fully tactile and features such as the title and some text are in Braille. The words of this text have been incorporated into an audio description which is available by telephoning on your mobile. The number to call is 0870 240 6094; choose option 2 and when asked for a pin number put in 201 and then hash. The use of the telephone in this way was a first in my experience and offers the advantages of overcoming the vandalism problem for sound equipment. It is

The queen unveils the panel

also available when you are feeling the panel and it allows people wherever they live, to listen in from home. This would be helpful if they are planning a visit to London so that they can decide where to visit. I include a brief example of the description taken from the audio guide:

Moving from left to right at the top of the panel there is a panoramic illustration of Parliament Square as it appears from where you are standing. Many of the buildings shown are in more detail below. A textured area, representing the road, marks a division of the two areas.

To hear the full audio description why not call the number quoted above and listen for yourself.

The panel also incorporates a tactile plan of the 14 mile walkway in central London established by the Trust in response to a request by Her Majesty the Queen to provide a welcoming insight for visitors into London life. This panel is located on that walkway.*

The royal car, flanked by police motor cycle outriders brought the Queen and Prince Philip from the Abbey direct to the panel. Her Majesty alighted from the car and with formal introductions over then pulled the tasselled cords on the cream coloured cover bearing the initials J W T with its crown logo. Her Majesty took quite some time exploring the panel for herself, with Isabella Murdoch, who is blind and Rebecca Elliot, the designer; she was interested in all aspects of the design and accessibility. The Queen was wearing an off-white coat with large wide brimmed hat to match, with black handbag, and shoes and white gloves.

Following inspection of the panel those involved with the project were introduced to Her Majesty. It was then that I had the honour of being introduced. I congratulated Her Majesty and taking my hand she thanked me and asked about my involvement with the project. The Duke of Edinburgh followed asking me questions about Wills, my Guide Dog and what part had he played. He leant towards me and we shared a joke about Wills. This was followed by an introduction to The Duke of Gloucester.

Introductions over, we were led by the Duke of Gloucester to the Westminster Abbey Crypt where the champagne reception was held during which the Duke of Gloucester took the opportunity to formally announce the Jubilee Greenway. The Greenway is a 60 mile route for walkers and cyclists which had been planned by the Jubilee Walkway Trust to connect all the Olympic venues in central London. In the same way, the Jubilee Walkway was created in celebration of the Queen's Silver Jubilee. It is hoped that this will be completed in time for the Olympics in 2012.

My involvement was that I work as a consultant with my friends of the Dog Rose Trust who specialise in the research and development of access systems. These help people who are blind and visually impaired to access and enjoy historic buildings, country walks and city and town walks. This is done using audio guides, tactile plans and models which often are universal so that they can be used by everyone. My involvement on this project was the audio description.

For further information go to www.jubileewalkway.com for the Jubilee Walkway Trust www.dogrose-trust.org.uk for the Dog Rose Trust.

* The panel in Parliament Square is the only one at present to have sound on it.

All my dogs, except Emma, have all met with royalty: Dorcas with the Duchess of Gloucester, Harry met Princess Anne who told me that he was so big he should have been fitted with a saddle not a harness and Wills who met Prince Phillip and the Queen in London as mentioned above. Emma's turn will surely come!